THE AMERICAN MUSEUM EXPERIENCE

In Search of Excellence

SCOTTISH MUSEUMS COUNCIL

Her Majesty's Stationery Office
Edinburgh

The Scottish Museums Council is an independent company, funded primarily by the Scottish Education Department, whose purpose is to improve the quality of local museum and gallery provision in Scotland. This it endeavours to do by providing a wide range of advice, services and financial assistance to its membership.

Scottish Museums Council
County House
20-22 Torphichen Street
Edinburgh
EH3 8JB

ISBN 0 11 492487 2

Foreword

Scottish museums are changing rapidly. There has been a very noticeable and quite unprecedented growth in the number of new museums opened in the last few years — many on a very ambitious scale — reflecting an expanding market for the museum experience. But a quieter, though no less significant, change has also been taking place — a change in the attitudes of those who manage our museums.

Running a successful museum nowadays requires a greater breadth of skills and knowledge than would have been the case even a decade ago. Having an expert knowledge of the collections is no longer enough. The fact that resources are getting harder to come by has changed all that.

Today's museum manager is expected to possess a far greater range of expertise. He must be no less of an expert in his subject matter. But increasingly he must be a populariser, a marketing man, an entrepreneur, a fund-raiser, a planner, a personnel manager and much more besides — or at least he must know when and how to call on these skills to maximise his museum's potential and efficiency.

This more rounded, professional approach to museum management contrasts with the traditional approach still found in most other European countries, where the emphasis on the curator solely as an expert on collections remains. In Britain, we have moved remarkably far and remarkably fast towards the American model of museum management and operations. So it was a natural step for the Scottish Museums Council to invite six leading members of the American profession to present their experience to a conference held during the Edinburgh International Festival in 1985.

The conference focussed on issues of particular current interest: fund-raising, education and management training. These themes were put into historical perspective and contemporary context by other papers examining the traditions and the future of the American museum movement.

The success of such an event is ultimately measured by the extent to which things change, and new ideas are put into practice. It has been argued that American society is so fundamentally different to our own that no transfer of experience is possible. And it is, of course, true that the American system is far more reliant on private sector funding than is our own, and that the scale of operations can be very large. Nevertheless, if we look for them, the similarities are certainly there too.

So what can we learn from the American museum experience?

For some of us, the emphasis on the need to discover and meet the public's real needs may be of particular interest. Or the ways in which "plural funding" is achieved. For others, it may be the clarity of purpose and the commitment to the planning process which strike a chord. Or the way in which the best American museums "harness the energy of the community".

But there is one thing which will cost us nothing at all. It is as relevant to the small museum as to the large, and to the public as well as the private sector museums. It is an attitude of mind — a commitment to excellence in all aspects of our museums' operations which, when coupled with imagination, determination and resourcefulness, can turn our visions into reality.

Graeme Farnell
Director
Scottish Museums Council

November 1985

Smithsonian Institution — the Castle and the Arts and Industries Building.

USA Museums in Context

Jane R. Glaser

Jane R. Glaser is Director of the Office of Museum Programs of the Smithsonian Institution which provides training activities, services, assistance, and information to museums in the United States and abroad. Previously Director of a Children's Museum and Planetarium for twelve years, Ms. Glaser served on the Council of the American Association of Museums (AAM) for eight years and is a Senior Examiner for the AAM Accreditation Commission. She serves as a museum consultant throughout the world and is a member of advisory committees of several museums, museums projects and museum studies programmes. She is secretary and board member of the International Council of Museums (ICOM) Committee on Training of Personnel, a member of the ICOM Advisory Committee and Chairperson of the US/GDR Subcommission on Museums for the International Research and Exchanges Board.

We are a vast country of assimilated immigrants who discovered a new land of curious wonders — our museums indeed reflect our unique history and development. Your former colonies shed their European cloaks, but cling to reminders of their origins and heritage. The history of American museums is in many ways the history of the people who settled in America.

Concisely, museum development in the U.S. may be best described in its various phases.

Phase One: the late 18th century with private, upper-class collections, no staff and miscellaneous display. In 1773, three years before the Declaration of Independence, the first public museum in the United States was founded at Charleston, S.C., and it remains in operation today. Private initiatives, not governmental authorities, representing a broad spectrum of social, intellectual and economic backgrounds, organized committees to start museums. There were successes and failures, but they undauntedly continued to establish, for the most part, natural science museums.

Historical societies were forming in the United States in seven states in the late 18th and early 19th centuries — all amassing collections of one sort or another. In 1785, Charles Wilson Peale, a portrait painter of renown, had an art gallery in his home and noticed that his visitors took great interest in his shells, minerals, and mounted birds. Thus was started the Peale Museum in Philadelphia for the purpose of displaying "natural curiosities".

Phase Two: in the first half of the 19th century there appeared "public" and institute collections of academies, universities, and learned societies; with some staff whose museum duties were secondary; a very general arrangement of objects; and an emphasis on research.

The Columbian Institute in Washington, D.C., was established in 1816 for the promotion of the arts and sciences, storing collections for the most part brought back by exploring expeditions.

While the first college art museum was founded at Yale in 1832, art mattered less than natural history in the early days of the United States whose people were pioneers in a new land seeking information that was immediately useful to them. Novelty and change were not unfamiliar to them and motivation to learn was a part of their daily lives.

The Smithsonian Institution was established in 1846, the result of a bequest of James Smithson, an Englishman and scientist, who had never visited the United States. The mandate from Mr. Smithson was that the Institution would serve "the increase and diffusion of knowledge among men". The interpretation of the ways in which knowledge was to be increased and disseminated was debated then and, in some quarters, is still debated today.

Phase Three: the second half of the 19th century, with public museums somewhat restricted; full-time staff not always paid; heavily classified typological exhibits; and continuing research.

The second half of the 19th century marked major changes in museums in the U.S. due both to the massive immigration from Europe and to the Industrial Revolution. Not only was there a growth of new museums, but attitudes changed and museums opened their doors to the "public" — the educational nature and responsibilities of museums took on greater importance. In New York, there was a new presence in the form of city tax support for museums and an edict that museums should be "as important and beneficial an agent in instruction of the people as any of the schools or colleges of the city". State governments were soon to follow suit.

Most of the important art museums in the U.S. were established in this period, including the Boston Museum of Fine Arts, Metropolitan Museum of Art, Chicago Art Institute, and Detroit Institute of Art. Significantly, private art collecting was abounding during the same period and future museum benefactors were appearing on the scene.

Louis Agassiz's dream of a museum that would be a "Library of the Works of God" was realized with the founding of the Gray Museum of Comparative Zoology at Harvard.

History museums consistently increased faster than all other kinds and do to this day. It was during this time that changes in governance in museums appeared and there was evidence that museums were becoming corporations governed by boards of trustees. Funds, as well as a volunteer work force, would be provided by individuals — American traditions continuing today. It was at this time also that

Brooklyn Children's Museum.

donations and chance accumulations. Constructive ideas came from George Brown Goode who wanted museums "to be transformed from 'bric-a-brac' cemeteries to nurseries of living thoughts and to retain their vitality in a continuous process of evolution". The goals of museums were yet to be clearly defined.

Museum architecture was dominated by the Beaux Arts Classicism style. Vital innovations in museum buildings did not begin to appear until the 1920's. Louis Sullivan urged his colleagues to "throw off the European past". Today, some new museum architectural styles are innovative and often dramatic; while others, interestingly, have made adaptive use of the 19th and early 20th century structures.

educational exhibitions and co-operation with schools marked the emergence of "public service" as opposed to "club activity". National parks, state parks, and historic landmarks began to share educational responsibilities.

Phase Four: the first half of the 20th century with museums truly for the general public; an emphasis on elementary and secondary education, a beginning phase of professionalism (the American Association of Museums was organized), organization and paid staff, and the first phase of interpretive exhibitions with period rooms, habitats, demonstrations, and outdoor museums; a decline in research.

An expansion period for U.S. museums was underway, the modern museum scene was set. Museum exhibitions were still done somewhat haphazardly and sometimes seemed incomprehensible to the visitor. Acquisitioning was not done in an orderly manner, but was mostly the result of

Improving transportation brought greater numbers of visitors to museums; larger museums began lending collections to smaller ones and schools received objects for the first time. Out-of-the-way historic house museums received visitors due to the increased number of automobiles and improved roads.

Phase Five: the second half of the 20th century, with efforts to attract and to popularize; to provide services for the disadvantaged and special audiences; more intense attention to professionalism with specialization and trained staffs; and expansion of interpretive exhibitions with audio-visuals, guides, living history, computers, participatory and interactive exhibits; research strengthened.

Progress in museums in the U.S. was impressive between the two World Wars. Francis H. Taylor, in *Babel's Tower, The Dilemma of the Modern Museum* said, "the American Museum is neither an abandoned

The late 1920's saw the acceptance of contemporary art in the U.S.A.

European palace nor a solution for storing national wealth … It is an American phenomenon developed by the people, for the people, and of the people." However, there was still a conflict of ideas having to do with the educational role of museums. There were those who viewed museums as "social instruments", those who concluded that museums were a definite "educational force, contributing to the economic and cultural life of their communities"; conversely, some questioned an educational effort as a panacea for all the ills of society and others believed every object of art should communicate to the spectator with as little interference as possible.

An increase in museum attendance aroused questioning concerning numbers as reliable indicators of quality, excellence, and success. The doubters were outnumbered and the surge of conducted tours, loan collections, lectures, and museum clubs continued. Period rooms, dioramas, habitat groups, and models of machines and specimens flourished, reaching a miscellaneous variety of people from all walks of life. The "living history" or total environment museum appeared; examples were Colonial Williamsburg, a result of the beneficence of John D. Rockefeller, Jr., and Greenfield Village, established by Henry Ford; both were evidence of the continuation of private initiative in supporting museums.

New York's Museum of Modern Art (MOMA), founded in 1929, laid the groundwork for the acceptance of contemporary art in the United States.

The National Gallery of Art in Washington, D.C., opened its doors in 1941, a gift to the United States from Andrew W. Mellon. Other donors followed suit, with collections based on the same standards of excellence stipulated by Mr. Mellon.

This period also saw the use of museum memberships among average American citizens, who thereby were able to enjoy special benefits and privileges at a reasonable rate.

It was also during this time that a few psychologists took notice of museums to assess the learning experiences of museum visitors and the relationship between exhibitions and resultant learning and enjoyment. Edward D. Robinson, of Yale University, initiated studies in the late twenties that led to the more recent research and evaluation of visitor behaviour.

Alma Wittlin, in *Museums: In Search of a Useable Future*, said it was
> "a time for meandering questions more than for definite answers: what indeed were the primary functions of museums? Did all museums have to follow the pattern of a uniform purpose? If museums did not exist, would people of the twentieth century feel the need to invent them?"

All of the questions above have been examined and re-examined, with new ones added since 1945. We continue to seek answers, but museums in the U.S. have taken "giant steps" during the last four decades toward professionalism, quality, integrity, and indeed *excellence*.

In quantitative terms, the museums in the U.S. have shown enormous growth. In the 1960s a new museum was founded every 3.3 days, and today there are approximately 6,000 museums. The most recent growth occurred before and during the Bicentennial in 1976 when communities, searching for their historical identities, established museums to tell stories of local pride. The museum universe expanded from the traditional art, history, and natural history disciplines to art and science centres, nature centres, zoos, botanical gardens, planetariums, aquariums, and children's museums.

Incidentally, children's museums, an American phenomenon, actually trace back to 1899 when the Brooklyn Children's Museum was founded. Over one hundred such institutions now offer youth and family-orientated exhibitions and activities. Pioneers in contemporary education appealing to the otherwise neglected tactile senses, children's museums offer a special kind of motivating learning environment.

U.S. cultural pluralism, during these decades, has resulted in a multitude of ethnic museums including Hispanic, Jewish, African-American, and Native American institutions. Ethnicity, identification, and preservation of cultural heritage have emerged, and there are today over 125 African-American and 100 Native American museums.

New technologies have created a need and are the focus of attention in museums of radio, television, holography, computers, photography, American crafts, and space exploration.

Appealing to all segments of its population, the United States has created museums of railroads, electricity, maritime artifacts, jails, folk art, deserts, the military, canals, coal, oil, fire, sports, decorative arts, and most recently women's art and the holocaust.

Some geographical areas of the United States with shifting populations, such as the southwest and Florida, have shown a particularly rapid growth in museums.

According to the American Association of Museums publication *Museums for a New Century*, since 1964, 30 new art museums have been built or are in the advanced stages of planning in the western states, and the number of all types of museums in Texas has increased sixfold in the last 15 years — from 106 to more than 650. Florida has produced 30 new museums since 1964, an increase of 67% in 20 years.

There are few reliable statistics on visitor attendance at American museums. In the last decade, however, museums have made a far greater effort than before to attract audiences and there has been a boom in attendance. A survey in 1980 indicated that 68% of Americans go to museums, 3% higher than the number who go to sports events. I suspect that in 1985 the percentage has grown. At the Smithsonian alone, with its 13 museums, there were approximately 27 million visitors last year. However, we might consider the warning of A.E. Parr, that

"Living History" at Greenfield Village, Michigan.

"the grossness of a purely quantitative self-esteem may also back-fire in the end. It should not be forgotten that the Roman circuses likewise enjoyed excellent attendance records. The question is not how many arrive, but how well they are served by what they find when they get there."

At this juncture it is perhaps timely to remind those not already aware of the fact that the approximately 6,000 institutions in the United States that make up the museum universe are largely independent entities and not part of any governmental or organized system. They are, as I have pointed out, extremely diverse in discipline and also widely divergent in size, governance, and their sources of funding. A majority of American museums are governed by private voluntary boards of trustees who serve as policymakers and often fund-raisers, as well as having the right of approval of the budgets of their institutions. These boards are subject to the laws of their states having to do with non-profit charitable organizations. There are approximately 2,000 museums operated by governmental units, for the most part at state, county, or municipal levels. The federal government supports National Park Service museums, presidential libraries/museums, and about 60-65% of the Smithsonian Institution's budget. Such government support funds are raised from public taxes, but those same museums usually depend heavily upon private support as well. Another substantial number of museums are constituent parts of colleges and universities.

Over half American museums are history museums, including historic houses and sites; living history farms and villages; and state, county, and city historical institutions. The next largest discipline group in numbers, but the largest in attendance and budget, are science museums, which include natural history, science and technology centres, planetariums, aquariums, zoos, and botanical gardens. Art museums, publicity to the contrary, rank third in both attendance and numbers.

A 1978 study, the most recent statistical survey, indicated that roughly 4% of the museums included had budgets in excess of $1,000,000 and nearly 75% had annual operating budgets below $100,000.

The size and scope of American museums must be considered and understood in order to examine their quest for excellence. It is important to note here their growth and development without any national policy, uniformity of rules or regulations, or centralization of any type. Obviously, there are advantages and disadvantages, strengths and weaknesses in such a system. Jealously guarding their independence and autonomy, museums have enormous opportunities for innovation, creativity, and flexibility. Without central controls, bureaucratization and delays may be minimized and problem-solving and decision-making become more imaginative with numerous possibilities for change and long-range planning.

On the other hand, duplicate effort may exist, and lack of national statistics and collections data, and dependable funding sources are shortcomings that are deterrents to the search for excellence.

Nonetheless, there is no mechanism for a central authority and, I suspect, little desire for one. As a result, numerous voluntary professional associations have assumed a prominent role in promulgating the mission of museums. The American Association of Museums (AAM), founded in 1906, is the "umbrella" organization, with a membership in 1985 of over 1800 institutions and 6,400 individuals. Others include the American Association of State and Local History, the Association of Science and Technology Centers, the Association of Art Museum Directors, the College Art Association, the Art Museums Association, the Science Museums Directors Association, and Regional and State Associations.

In its "search for excellence", the museum community in the United States is also attempting to define itself and its parameters. The 1968 Belmont Report, a study of U.S. museums, accounted for their quantity and services, and expressed concern for the need to set standards. The Belmont Report urged "that the AAM and its member institutions develop and agree upon acceptable criteria and methods of accrediting museums". In 1970, the AAM established a Museum Accreditation programme. After a careful examination and identification of all the functions and characteristics of museums, it employed a self-evaluation and peer review process to assure standards for professionalism.

With the start of accreditation, for the first time in its history, the museum profession in the United States had measurable standards for institutions. The AAM proposed a definition of "museums" to determine the types of institutions eligible for accreditation:
"For the purposes of the accreditation programme of the AAM, a museum is defined as an organized and permanent non-profit institution, essentially educational or aesthetic in purpose, with professional staff, which owns and utilizes tangible objects, cares for them and exhibits them to the public on some regular schedule."

After committee deliberations for over two years, the AAM membership accepted the basic definition with additional clarification suggesting that "professional staff" meant a profession relevant to museology and to the museum's discipline and a capability for scholarship; that "educational" required the "knowledgeable utilization" of objects through exhibitions and interpretation.

Thus the examination of the commonality of functions in museums would better serve the search for standards, quality, and excellence than other more superficial criteria. Joseph V. Noble, Director of the Museum of the City of New York, in an article entitled "Museum Manifesto", declared, in no order of priority, that:
"The five responsibilities — acquisition, conservation, study, interpretation and exhibition — are, of course, interrelated; together they form an entity. They are like the five fingers of a hand, each independent but united for a common purpose. If a museum omits or slights any of these five responsibilities, it has handicapped itself immeasurably, and I seriously doubt whether such a museum will survive in the challenging years that lie ahead. Conversely, if we each strengthen our own institutions in these five inseparable areas, we will fulfill our obligations to the past and present and our aspirations for the future."

Since 1970, the Accreditation Commission has regularly assessed, revised, and strengthened its guidelines and has added definitions for accreditation of planetariums, science and technology centres, art centres, historic sites, zoos, botanical gardens, and aquariums. A re-accreditation programme, for those museums first accredited in the 1970s, was established in the early '80s to assure the maintenance of the standards and criteria.

A new vision of the museum's role in society emerged along with a renewed sense of responsibility to preserve and transmit cultural values to the community of humankind.

The methods, skills, techniques, and practices utilized to fulfill these roles varies as greatly as there are types, disciplines and sizes of museums in the United States. The diversity of museum goals, objectives, and organization reflects the diversity of American society. As interests, directions, and activities shift, sometimes the character of the museum shifts as well. Differing from schools and libraries, museums are pliable social institutions and appear to move in several directions at the same time.

Let's examine, for a few moments, the various aspects of U.S. museum operations and functions and the search for excellence, and from that perhaps we can detect some reasons for the immense popularity of museums in the United States today; for the perception of excellence may risk change with popularization.

The barometer for the search for excellence may be found in the trends of the five basic functions of museums.

COLLECTING
In the last two decades, collecting and management of collections have had increased attention due partly to a surge of self-examination by museums and perhaps

also due to an awareness of the problems revealed through new literture on acquisition, de-accessioning, data control, and maintenance written by concerned museum professionals. Storage, documentation, conservation, security, and the need for adequately trained personnel have captured the interest of those who had in the past concentrated primarily on amassing collections. Somewhat jolted from apathy and neglect, the U.S. museum field turned its attention to new developments in scientific conservation treatment, to the application of computer technology for data management, to modern equipment available for storage facilities, and to the proliferation of university museum studies programmes for training museum professionals.

It was apparent that a renewal of ethical standards was required. The 1924 Code of Ethics was no longer relevant and an AAM Committee formulated a new document, *Museum Ethics*, in 1978. The Curators Committee followed suit with a more specific code of ethics for curatorial conduct, and they are exploring now the possibilities for individual certification.

Both ethical and legal constraints associated with collections management had an impact on acquisition practices for discrimination, relevance, purpose, system, and documentation. Most United States museums depend heavily upon gifts or bequests to acquire the major parts of their collections, especially since the present tax laws encourage donors to give objects; but ethical and legal standards are applied to donations as well as to purchases made by a museum. Conflict of interest laws affect staff and trustees who are private collectors, but who purchase for the museum as well.

Many museums now have clearly stated collections policies, which include the problems and dangers of de-accessioning. While often undertaken to "upgrade" or eliminate poor choices of objects and artifacts, this practice is sometimes mistakenly used to acquire funds, or for personal taste. Some museums now have policies to de-accession only to other museums.

Computer data control, in the hands of the unskilled, may be disastrous. It is recognized that competent registrars or collections managers should be responsible for correlation of the information for proper automated record-keeping. U.S. museums are experiencing "growing pains" as technology advances at a rapid pace and the field is attempting to keep up and indeed to catch up, with major efforts toward computerizing collections.

Security systems have become quite sophisticated in the major museums in the United States, but as for fire protection, experts still debate on the pros and cons of using sprinkler systems or halon. Alarm systems are prevalent but expensive, and many museums depend upon trained guards, badges, and limited access to collections. Art thefts have become of international concern and, as in some other countries, the Federal Bureau of Investigation in the U.S. has an "art squad" for investigation, apprehension, and recovery. The International Foundation for Art Research in New York City maintains an archive of stolen objects and publishes a journal with current listings and some illustrations.

The trend towards collecting for the 20th century in the United States is sometimes criticized, but more often accepted as a necessary link to the past for future generations. Selectivity and discrimination in collecting may avoid the hazards of numbers of insignificant objects, and standards are still being established.

CONSERVATION

The obligation of museums to preserve their collection is a monumental responsibility; but the voices of the conservators and other concerned museum professionals are being heard throughout our land. As I have mentioned, without a national policy, each museum sets its own programmatic and financial priorities. Each museum with its own discipline, purpose, collections, and functions has to decide on its individual commitments. However, the American Institute for the Conservation of Historic and Artistic Works (AIC) and the National Institute for the Conservation of Cultural Property (NIC), both voluntary professional organizations, are major forces of concern for professional conservation standards and express their views through national publications, conferences, and meetings. The AIC adopted a revised *Code of Ethics and Standards of Practice* in 1979 as the accepted standards for conservation in the United States. The NIC identifies and reports major needs and problems, offers recommendations for solutions, recommends policies and programmes, and has recommended the creation of a National Institute of Conservation. Along with the AAM, the three organizations are co-operating in a commissioned study to develop strategies for the organization, maintenance, and conservation of museum collections, and to strengthen the funding efforts for

Second half of 19th century: a historic landmark: Morse-Libby House.

conservation by private and federal agencies. For the first time, the Institute of Museum Services (IMS) was authorized in 1984 to spend $2.85 million on competitive grants to museums for collections surveys and treatment, environmental controls, conservation, research, and training. The Director of IMS recently lamented at a public meeting, however, that not enough proposals are being submitted for surveys of collections and for preventive care. She questioned, "How can you spend good money to preserve an object and then put it back into the identical environment that damaged it to begin with? Shouldn't the number one priority be examination of the collection?"

Other federal agencies provide conservation-related competitive grants, but funds available for the hundreds of proposals are inadequate to meet the needs.

Conservation treatment services are provided in four ways: 1) freelance professional conservators; 2) conservation treatment facilities located within museums and providing services only for those institutions (an estimated 50 in number); 3) conservation treatment facilities located within museums also providing services to others (approximately 10 of these); and, 4) co-operative conservation organizations contracting their services, usually as regional centres.

Since 1960, four university-based conservation training programmes have been established awarding advanced degrees after three or four years of intensive classroom study and laboratory work. Conservators, no longer regarded as mere technicians, are now recognized as highly skilled professionals with specialized knowledge necessary for the care, handling, loan, and treatment of museum objects.

There is now an awareness of the need to bridge the gap between conservation and its applied scientific support. Too few conservation laboratories can afford the costs of scientific research, but the numbers are increasing. There is anticipation that these efforts will be strengthened with the opening of the J. Paul Getty Conservation Institute in Los Angeles, for pure and applied research that will benefit the conservation field throughout the world.

Preventive care of collections is probably the most neglected area of conservation and collections management — a universal problem. Conservators and curators alike agree that preventive maintenance through proper handling, storage, environmental controls, and exhibiting is of primary importance, but, again, the backlog of amassed collections, financial constraints, and lack of training are deterents to progress. However, the U.S. is beginning to deal with these problems through vocal outcries from conservators, awareness training for non-conservators, relevant literature, and more funding. It will be a long, uphill struggle.

RESEARCH

Research efforts in U.S. museums, for the most part, are collections-based to ascertain the authenticity, origin, and larger context of the objects, occupying a large percentage of the work time of most curators. Ever since our earliest museums, there have been serious debates as to the role of the museum in education or research. Joseph Henry, the first Secretary of the Smithsonian Institution, noted that there were "thousands of institutions actively engaged in the diffusion of knowledge in our country, but not a single one which gives direct support to its increase. Knowledge can only be increased by original research, which requires patient thought and laborious and often expensive experiments."

However, the public role of museums expanded and basic research declined until there was a renewed interest in the 20th century in fieldwork and use of live specimens in the natural sciences as well as in the data bases offered by research in the fields of anthropology and archaeology.

Art museums lead in research to authenticate objects and for conservation of collections. Originally having goals only for the edification and uplift of citizens through exhibitions, art museums have turned their attention to scholarly research for authentication and publication.

History museums provide a unique environment for objects. The evolution of the place of research in them has been a slow process because of the traditional documentation of history in the written word by academic historians. However, in recent years attention has been focused on "social history" of past and present societies whereby the object takes on a new significance in basic historical research. Material culture and oral history projects attest to the fact that museums may sometimes be the only sources of knowledge about past accomplishments.

In most museums the balancing act between research and educational obligations continues to this day. Almost fifty years ago, Lawrence V. Coleman wrote:

> "Like institutions of higher education, museums are likely to be as deep or shallow in their teaching as they are strong or weak in research. Where there is no spirit of inquiry there can be but limited learning since the scholar is a product of the habit of investigation. Where teaching goes unrefreshed by learning, it soon becomes uninformed and even sooner dull."

Harold Skramstad states that "it is interesting to note that in the United States those museums with strong research programmes generally are leaders in the field of museum education as well." I would add that there may be some notable exceptions.

The curator as researcher and scholar today is a communicator, who not only publishes, but is part of a team, a subject matter expert, attempting to meet other museum goals and objectives. Discipline and expertise are required to assist in planning and producing exhibitions as well as working co-operatively with other staff for interpretation and public programming. The team approach is taking on new importance and is being promoted widely among U.S. museums today. The old conflicts are gradually dissolving.

Again, depending upon the priorities and size of the individual museums, the amount of time for basic research varies from only basic documentation time to sabbaticals for personal research. Budgets and special grants for financial support affect the amount of scholarly contributions that museums may make. There are a variety of funding sources, both federal and private, and government contracts to solve specific applied research problems.

There is considerable collaboration among researchers with staff in other museums as well as with colleagues in universities and other research-orientated institutions. There are joint academic appointments, fellowships, internships, and university advanced-degree programmes for museum studies that include a heavy emphasis on specific disciplines. Researchers in museums continue to publish, not only their scholarly monographs and books, but collections catalogues and contributions to museum journals such as *Curator, Museum News,* and the *Museum Studies Journal.*

EXHIBITIONS
Written standards of excellence for museum exhibitions in the United States do not exist. This does not mean, however, that there are neither superior exhibitions nor that there is no effort towards excellence. It means merely that there are no special rules, regulations, or authoritative judgements on design and production. Individualism reigns supreme.

In its own way, this has provided enormous space for creativity, innovation, and

imagination. Techniques used thirty years ago are no longer valid, as the expectations of the visitors have changed. The diversity of presentation of objects and concepts has demonstrated that communication with the public is foremost, and that the intrinsic, as well as the extrinsic value of objects and artifacts provides for "display in context". No longer shown among rows and rows of items with simple labels, rarely is a solitary piece complete unless it is presented in its original or current context or in the context of its relationships to other pieces. Museum exhibitions present life-size dioramas, depictions of the origin and use of objects, recreations of life styles through room settings, live habitats, and outdoor living history; participatory areas for experiential and "hands-on" environments; and visible storage. Many exhibitions are enhanced with the use of audio-visuals, computers, and video-disc displays.

Audio-visuals took hold in the late 60s, were over-used and abused for a number of years, and now appear to be taking their proper place as supplementary to the presentation of objects and specimens. Films, videotapes, and slide-tape programmes are providing information and interpretation that brings the context of objects into full view beyond the immediate scene. There are still dangers in over-use that may detract from the real purpose of museums. Entertainment vs. education continues to be discussed and debated in many quarters.

U.S. museums are experimenting with computers in exhibitions — in science centres and in children's museums quite successfully. The video-disc, still somewhat experimental and expensive, has potential for visitor access to vast collections not otherwise seen.

South Street Seaport Museum, New York.

Exhibition loans, a very positive means of collaboration among museums, are a mainstay of many small museums who cannot afford to mount their own exhibits or change them often. The art and science disciplines in museums are leaders in sharing their well-researched and educative exhibitions. Independent organizations and associations have been founded in the last twenty years to provide a variety of exhibitions to museums, at an affordable price, otherwise not available to them.

The special exhibitions sometimes referred to as "blockbusters" are a recent phenomenon that have their advocates and detractors. Great collections never before viewed have caused excitement and massive public response unprecedented in U.S. museums. Primarily seen in art museums, although sometimes ethnographic in content, the "blockbuster" has generated new income and new audiences. The doubters caution that these

are too temporary for a lasting effect on museum audiences and that museums must be wary of becoming dependent on them, sacrificing their basic purpose. The definitions of "success" with exhibitions vary as U.S. museums vary, as the public appetite enlarges, and as museums become a basic amenity of life in the United States.

EDUCATION AND INTERPRETATION
Since the 1940s, U.S. museums have been committed to establishing broader and livelier programmes of education; they have been questioning and examining how people learn in museums and the educational potential of museums. Responsible for presenting not only information, but ideas as well, museums are identifying their audiences and seeking to reach out to the changing and diverse populations in their communities. Museum-school partnerships, including teacher-training, are the rule in American museums with thousands of school children attending demonstrations, lectures, classes, and a myriad of activities; more recently there is increased attention to adult audiences through films, lectures, classes, and performances.

The educational significance of museums has been gaining prominence and scope. Today most museums in the U.S. endeavour to narrate a coherent story through their collections, to stimulate the visitor toward exploration, discovery, wonder, and learning to "see" by their experiences; and to provide other enrichment and educational activities.

The museum has become a place that provides opportunities for everyone, reaching out to new and special audiences irrespective of age, education, or economic levels. S. Dillon Ripley, former Secretary of the Smithsonian Institution, in his book *The Sacred Grove,*

In the early 19th century there were few art museums: the first College Art Museum at Yale.

said, "somewhere within these realms there are clues to our understanding of ourselves and I suspect, our survival."

Museums in the United States recognise their role as communicators, retaining their basic functions of collecting and preserving, for the advantage of society. They are striving to maintain a quality of excellence, ethical standards, and an assurance of integrity as communicators — no easy task. The museum uniquely provides an opportunity for communication between the visitors and the objects, for seeing in new ways with new perceptions, and for "experiencing" in a different learning environment from schools, universities, and libraries. In today's "learning society," which attempts to understand patterns of learning and strives for significantly new and higher levels of instruction, the educational potential of

museums is enormous. Their extraordinary resources are a challenging prospect to those responsible for expanding public access and public knowledge.

Museums as learning resources are searching for excellence and examining new inter-disciplinary and innovative ways to set standards for the future that will improve the quality of life for all people.

There appears to be a growing recognition that all museums' functions have an educational purpose in one manner or another, and that all museums should be encouraged to make a specific contribution to that end.

Let me quote four examples. First, most of the treasures held by museums are in storage, rarely examined or viewed by anyone beyond the museum staff and visiting scholars. Access to these collections, without causing irreparable damage, is taking form through visible storage, object libraries, public study centres, and hands-on inter-active activities, exhibitions, and programmes.

Second, publications by curators are becoming increasingly marketable to the general public as well as to academic colleagues.

Third, museums are conceptualizing and planning exhibitions to communicate educational information as well as to entertain and be aesthetically pleasing. They may be multi-dimensional utilizing sight, sound, taste, touch, hearing, and other perceptions as vehicles to convey meaning. Exhibitions may be passive with an indirect response, or may actively involve visitors in their explorations and investigations.

Fourth, traditionally the museum educator has been assigned the interpretive responsibilities and understands the basic why's and how's in the conceptual development of programmes. The educator organizes outreach activities with loan kits, staff visits, and demonstrations for schools, for the elderly, the disabled, and other special audiences. The educator is expected to systematically observe, analyze, and understand audiences, and is often a member of a planning group for exhibitions, providing an important and dynamic link with the public.

New and informative publications for schools, libraries, universities, and the general public are being produced and disseminated by museums as disciplinary learning tools and for intellectual participation by more than a select few. There is renewed effort in the United States for a sense of community and responsiveness; an effort to collaborate with other museums, other cultural, and educational institutions, and with the business and governmental communities; a desire for the sharing of information and resources, exchanging of personnel, collections, and exhibitions, and publicizing of programming; all these factors contribute immeasurably to the educational impact and vitality of museums. Alliances, collaboratives, and consortia have been organized and are thriving in many communities.

If we perceive museums as learning resources where anyone may participate at his or her own pace and level of learning, and if we have the sensitivity to clarify issues, then all who work in museums are indeed educators.

This does not mean that there are no problems or issues confronting U.S. museums as educational institutions.

In U.S. museums today there is an ongoing search for museum educational theory, for definitions of non-formal education, and for relationships with other educational institutions. There is continuing inquiry into changing populations as museum audiences, into changing educational patterns and trends, and into the use of new technologies.

We continue to re-examine and debate museums' educational role, for that is the nature of the profession, but perhaps standards may evolve as guidelines toward uncompromising excellence for all who are concerned with the quality of life and life-long learning.

While there is a demand for an increase in public services there is also a decrease in public funds. The equation remains to be resolved with increasing competition for limited resources and pressure to work constructively together.

Museum "educators" continue in their determination to be recognized and respected as professionals in a field where the curator has been the dominant "professional."

The director's role in supporting the educative aspects of museums remains a questionable one in many museums, but, hopefully, that is changing and educational policies may be established in museums in the future just as they have been for collecting.

The issue of attracting minority and special audiences to U.S. museums remains a major concern. Museums are examining their programmes and exhibitions for relevance to the elderly, the disabled, and ethnic audiences; and are exploring avenues of entry into the profession for minorities.

For the past fifteen years there has been a renewed interest and involvement in museum evaluation in order to understand visitor behaviour and experience as well as to research the learning that occurs in museums. Many museums believe significant benefits have resulted from efforts to determine their effectiveness, but others express scepticism about the value of formal evaluation.

GENERAL

There are contemporary issues and concerns facing U.S. museums, including: the business person or the university president as the director of a museum as opposed to a person from the discipline; presentation of controversial subjects in museum exhibitions when there is a public outcry; the return of objects and artifacts to their people or countries of origin; trustee and staff conflicts in terms of responsibilities; museums studies training versus the academic discipline; continued expansion of the old and creation of possibly too many new museums; and the ever-present one, is there a museum profession?

The discussion of museum "professionalism" continues and as recently as the June 1985 meeting of the AAM, the question was debated interminably. The issue is often confused, as many equate museum "professionalism" with a museum "profession." Arguments ensue that a museum profession does not exist nor should it, while others state that the concepts of museology must be broader and that there is a body of knowledge and literature that indeed comprises a unique "profession." On the other hand, "professionalism" is based on ethics and standards of performance and museum people can indeed agree on that common goal toward excellence. The accreditation system defines professional standards, but until more than 600 eligible U.S. museums are accredited, we industriously pursue "professionalism" through self-study and more stringent standards.

Other critical aspects of U.S. museum operations include:

1) Development and/or fund-raising which requires a major portion of the time of the director, staff, and trustees of museums. In an effort to solve the problem many large and medium size museums now hire development officers. A private national Business Committee for the Arts has encouraged corporate philanthropy and is partially easing the task of museum fund raisers.

2) Public relations and "marketing" have taken on new definitions and importance in "selling" our museums to their communities. Radio and television programmes along with direct mail, newspapers, and journals provide museum visibility as never before.

3) Museum shops exist in every museum to produce income and are carefully monitored to carry only museum-related merchandise. Large museums develop their own unique products to enhance their sales. Earned income is now quite acceptable and even crucial to a museum's existence and survival.

4) U.S. museums could not exist without the huge numbers of dedicated and talented volunteers who give tours, serve as receptionists, exhibition preparators, research assistants, clerical help, and fulfill a multitude of other museum responsibilities.

5) Growing membership in U.S. museums provides not only income, but community support. Other auxiliary organizations such as "friends" and guilds are support groups that are actively involved in museum fund-raising activities.

6) Graduate museum studies programmes have proliferated to the extent that guide-

In the second half of the 19th century major art museums were established.

lines and standards for review and self-study have been written by an AAM Museum Studies Committee, but the effectiveness is yet to be measured.

7) Museum staff are uniformly underpaid, but, for the most part, committed and dedicated professionals.

8) After examining their cost-effectiveness, an increasing number of museums are charging admission to finance increasing costs, with no demonstrated negative effect on attendance.

9) Participatory management or democratization of museums in many U.S. museums has increased productivity and opportunities for independent thought and action. Management of museums remains a concern while training for managers has increased with workshops, institutes, and courses.

10) Most U.S. museums today have an international consciousness that broadens their perspectives and promises new collaboration.

11) Women's voices are being raised and being heard as they protest the limited opportunities for leadership of major U.S. museums. There will be a national conference in 1986 on "Women's Changing Roles in Museums" at the Smithsonian.

Where one stands affects our convictions and determines our priorities, and how we look at things depends on our vantage point. Nonetheless, the possibility of relating to you the American museum experience represented a challenge to me to consider, I hope objectively, an area that binds us together in our endeavours. There is great commonality among museums the world over, for we share a commitment to collect and preserve, to research, to exhibit and interpret. Our systems and our cultures may differ, but there is a special value meeting together and sharing a variety of interests and viewpoints.

There may not be unanimous agreement on the nature of the U.S. museum profession as I have described it, or a preferred method of dealing with current issues and problems, but there surely exists an enthusiastic commitment to a healthy and dynamic climate for museums in the United States.

*Dallas Museum of Art, with
downtown Dallas beyond.*

The New Dallas Museum of Art

Harry S. Parker

Harry S. Parker III became Director of the Dallas
Museum of Art in 1974, having previously served in
the Education Department of the Metropolitan
Museum of Art in New York, becoming Vice-Director
for Education in 1971.

He is a past-President of the Association of Art
Museum Directors.

The Dallas Museum of Art is a public institution created in 1903 and owned by the City of Dallas. Its first home was built in 1936 on the outskirts of downtown in Fair Park. The 64,000 square foot facility eventually inhibited development and expansion of the collections and the Museum's services. The new facility opened on January 29th 1984, with a total of 210,000 square feet, almost tripling the space available at the old site. Located on an 8.9 acre site, the new Dallas Museum of Art is the catalyst and cornerstone of the planned Arts District that will encompass a 60-acre site on the northern edge of the central business district. In addition to the Museum, the Arts District includes a concert hall and a theatre centre; a high school for the arts; several historic buildings; parks, plazas, fountains; retail and commercial space; 10 million square feet of office space, major hotels, and residential units.

The primary impetus behind the Museum building programme was a $24.8 million bond issue approved by Dallas voters in a November 6th 1979 election. This historic vote represents the greatest amount of funding ever raised for a cultural project by public referendum in the United States. An additional $27.6 million has been raised from private sources, making the funding drive for the Museum the largest amount ever raised in Dallas for a cultural institution. The two funding campaigns demonstrate the strong partnership between public and private sectors present in Dallas. Approximately $50 million of the funds went towards land acquisition, construction costs, fees, and equipment.

American tax laws encourage private sector contributions by making such gifts deductible from the base income against which taxes are calculated. For high income donors, the government, in effect, currently "pays" as much as one-half of the contribution. Needless to say, this is an incentive to generosity, but not the only motivation. Dallasites were equally stimulated by a strong sense of civic pride and eager to establish cultural facilities comparable to those of older cities and, particularly, current rivals such as

Children in the Gateway Gallery, Dallas Museum of Art.

Houston and Fort Worth. Museums are further judged to make a quantitative contribution to a city's appeal to tourism and convention business, as a lure to new corporations and prospective employees considering re-location to Dallas, and as a stimulus to the value of adjoining commercial properties — adding to the property tax base of the community. In these ways, the museum is "good for business".

ARCHITECTURAL STYLE
The style of the new museum is plain, that is a conscious effort to underplay the facility in favour of the presentation of the art. The galleries are white with a minimum of obstruction from lighting fixtures, air conditioning duct work, or, indeed, anything else. Natural light is used but controlled. Floor surfaces vary from wood to stone to wool; all colours are muted. Spaces are well proportioned and varied with a high central space for presentation of large-scale contemporary art and more intimate galleries for traditional painting and sculpture. Sunlit,

open-to-the-air courts are introduced for visual relief from the art experience. Comfortable seating, flower arrangements, water and lilies are integrated to vary the visual stimuli.

Architect Edward Larrabee Barnes has designed several art museums including the Walker Art Center in Minneapolis, the Scaife Wing of the Carnegie Museum in Pittsburg, and the Asia Society in New York. The new Dallas Museum incorporates many of the features of his other museum work and notably continues the smooth and easy flow of space which so identifies his work. Outdoor spaces are integrated with interiors; flexibility is combined with a sense of permanence. Although the architecture is plain and non-competitive with the art, it is not weak. One is aware of spatial organization in a classic beaux arts frame, of repeated architectural references and, principally, of a solid practical scheme. It has been deemed "user friendly" by *Time Magazine* and "picture friendly" by visiting curators, because it is both pleasant and satisfying. It does work well. Over half the space is directed to behind-the-scenes activities ranging from loading dock with overview from security, registration, and receiving to the spacious library and slide library, attractive office spaces and expansive storage.

NEW COMMISSIONS
For the new building, the Museum commissioned major works of art, including a large-scale steel work by Ellsworth Kelly, installed in a specially created site in the Sculpture Garden. The Sculpture Garden also contains Scott Burton's *Granite Settee*. And Richard Fleischner designed, created, and installed the Education Courtyard. Claes Oldenburg's *Stake Hitch*, shaped like a giant stake "hammered" into the floor, provides a

dramatic focal point in the 40-foot barrel vault which houses the Museum's growing contemporary collection. "Stake Hitch" is made of painted steel and aluminium, expanded foam, and reinforced resin. The "stake" itself rises 16 feet above the gallery floor and has a connecting "rope" to the top of the 40-foot vault. The lower portion of the

Barrel Vault with Stake Hitch *by Claes Oldenburg, Dallas Museum of Art.*

stake descends 12 feet into the basement of the new Museum. The "rope" is 20 inches in diameter.

In a statement about the project, artist Oldenburg and his partner, Coosje van Bruggen, describe the concept of "Stake Hitch" and its aesthetic purpose:

> "The 'Stake Hitch' is both an attempt to embody certain attitudes and experiences concerning the place, Dallas, and to create a structure that simultaneously opposes and reinforces the design of the new Dallas Museum of Art.
>
> "The commission is treated as if it were an outdoor placement. It is an outdoor subject located indoors, as if the new Museum had been built over it. The scale of the sculpture was influenced by construction equipment seen within the Museum space during a visit, and construction equipment continues to be a strong presence in downtown Dallas.
>
> "The first idea for the project was a group of three long nails penetrating the vault of the Museum, in response to the architect's (Edward Larrabee Barnes) suggestion that something be done with the vaulted area to draw it into the rest of the space. The subject was then changed into a stake, and Coosje suggested that the stake should have a rope tied to it in a kind of cinematic-frame concept where the source to which the stake is attached is 'out of the picture'. When the stake was placed in the Museum space, the edge of the 'image' became the wall of the vault. The stake will appear to penetrate the floor into the loading platform in the basement, becoming a part of the architecture, and tying the levels of the

building together. The basement section of the stake may be seen from the street through the windows in the loading dock doors.

"The 'Stake Hitch' is an image of forces in tension, natural and human. There is the suggestion of raising a huge tent and of the form of a tornado — both events taking place in the large sky hidden from view, but to which the sculpture points.

"The rope is a basic form in many ways in Texas experience, especially the legendary

Part of the art collection.

kind, which could also be said of the sculpture's scale. A certain feeling of the outdoors and of country experience should be conveyed by the work in a rough way, to contrast with the refinement of the Museum."

THE COLLECTION
European Paintings and Sculpture
In the field of European paintings and sculpture, the main area of concentration is 18th, 19th, and 20th century art. A group of old master paintings includes fine examples by Procaccini, Paolini, Mignard, and Fabritius. A $5,000,000 bequest of purchase funds from Mrs. John B. O'Hara has permitted an ambitious collecting programme in 18th and 19th century art, and recent purchases from this fund include Courbet's important *Fox in the Snow*, Daumier's *Outside the Print-Sellers Shop*, a monumental Joseph Vernet entitled *Mountain Landscape with an Approaching Storm* and Bazille's poetic *Portrait of Paul Verlaine as a Troubadour*. Through such purchases the Museum plans to document the main historical currents leading to Impressionism, an area where holdings are already quite deep and will, it is hoped, eventually benefit further from distinguished private holdings in the community. For example, in the Impressionist field the Museum boasts important works by Manet, Monet, Pissaro, and Morisot; and from the Post-Impressionist period come paintings by Gauguin, Van Gogh, and Bernard as well as Redon, Vuillard, Bonnard, and Serusier. These late 19th century paintings are complemented by sculptures by Canova, Barye, Carpeaux, Rodin, Carrier-Belleuse and Degas, among others.

The early modern collections have considerable breadth but are distinguished

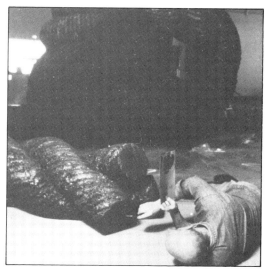

Mother and child working with Colour-Shape Game in the Gateway Gallery, Dallas Museum of Art.

Oldenburg signing The Stake Hitch, *Dallas Museum of Art.*

by two special concentrations, groups of eight paintings by Mondrian and three by Leger documenting different phases of their careers, all of which are gifts from the well known James and Lillian Clark collection. These are augmented by Brancusi's famous marble sculpture *Beginning of the World* and a large Matisse cut-out, as well as fine works by such artists as Kandinsky, Popova, Delaunay, Modigliani, Magritte, and Rouault. The collection of early modern sculpture covers most of the major stylistic developments of the period and includes fine examples by Maillol, Lipshitz, Gabo, Arp, Hepworth, Moore, and Giacometti. Thus a considerble spectrum is represented in one of the most revolutionary periods in all of art history.

Traditional American Art
The American art collection of the Dallas Museum of Art promises to be one of the most vital, growing areas of the new facility. The installation in the new galleries not only reflects the museum's increasing commitment to the presentation of important work by major American artists, but also acts as a centre for the study of the development of regional art.

The permanent collection in the museum is strong in key areas, generally anchored by a few major works. This is certainly the case with landscape painting, which includes the most famous American painting in the collection, Frederic Church's monumental masterwork, *The Icebergs*. Rediscovered several years ago, this work gained notoriety at auction and was presented to the museum by an anonymous donor. It is complemented by other outstanding examples of late 19th century landscape painting by George Inness, Alfred Bricher, Albert Bierstadt, Thomas Moran, and Alfred Jacob Miller. The museum collection is particularly strong in fine works of the turn of the century that reflect the influence of Impressionism. A large and beautiful view of *Springtime in Vermont* by Willard Leroy Metcalf is balanced by colourful examples by Childe Hassam, Maurice Prendergast, and Julian Alden Wier. Since Dallas is part of the greater Southwest, regional developments in landscape are well represented by the work of early Texas artists like Frank Reaugh and Edward G. Eisenlohr, and by the more modernist examples of the famous Taos colony of artists. Dallas was an important regionalist centre in the 1930's and 1940's, and the museum's holdings in that area are extensive; Alexandre Hogue's stark *Drouth Stricken Area*, painted in 1934, is a famous image. Paintings like Thomas Hart Benton's *Prodigal Son* or Edward Hopper's haunting *Lighthouse Hill* serve to round out the strong landscape holdings.

The Dallas Museum collection also includes fine examples of American portraiture, beginning with Gilbert Stuart's portraits of Mr. & Mrs. John Ashley, painted in 1799. There are other examples by Samuel Waldo, Chester Harding, and Thomas Sully. Mary Cassatt is represented by a soft and delicate pastel of a young mother and her child; Thomas Eakins, by a sensitive and introspective painting of Elizabeth Murray. The museum visitor can compare the brash and extrovert handling of John Singer Sargent's painting of a young girl with the softly modelled, almost Whistlerian portrait by William Merrit Chase of his favourite daughter. In terms of the 20th century, there is the magnificent portrait by George Bellows of his wife, Emma, as well as an imposing and texturally complex work by the noted Provincetown painter, Charles Hawthorne. Philip Evergood's portrait of his mother, on the other hand, is almost surrealistic for its wan, ethereal quality, while Andrew Wyeth's tempera of *That Gentleman* remains a favourite with museum visitors who enjoy its sense of mystery.

There are simple and elegant still lifes by William Hartnett, John F. Peto, and Emil Carlsen. In sculpture, there is the idealized beauty of Hiram Power's *America,* or the delicate abstraction of Alexander Calder's *Flower*. Gerald Murphy's magnificent machine-age abstract, *Watch*, heralds a small but potent selection of American modernist painting, which includes fine examples by Georgia O'Keeffe, Charles Demuth, and John Marin.

Post-World War II Art
The Dallas Museum of Art's collection of post-World War II art includes an outstanding representation of the major American artistic trends that have come to the fore since 1945. From the Abstract Expressionist period the Museum owns two highly important pictures by Jackson Pollock, an early 1947 drip painting, *Cathedral*, and *Portrait and A Dream* from 1953. Other significant works representing major figures involved with Abstract Expressionism are two Rothko paintings as well as individual works by Motherwell, Gottlieb, Still and Kline. A striking David Smith sculpture, *Cubi XVII*, represents the sculptural activity also occurring during this artistic period.

Two important Morris Louis paintings signifying his contribution to colour-field painting are included in the Museum's collection: *High*, 1959, an important transition piece from his series of "veils" to "unfurleds" and *Delta Gamma*, an "unfurled" from 1960.

Device, a 1961-62 work by Jasper Johns in which the artist combines his painterly technique with words and found objects in order to question our traditional aesthetic values, highlights the museum's collection of paintings from the 1960's.

Also during the 1960's proponents of Pop Art began to explore and exploit the contemporary world of advertising and commerce. Significant examples by artists working in this mode, such as Jim Dine, Tom Wesselman, and James Rosenquist, are included in the collection.

The Dallas Museum is especially rich in examples of geometric abstraction and the minimalist aesthetic. Outstanding paintings by Robert Mangold, Brice Marden and Al Held reinforce sculptural statements by Tony Smith, Robert Morris, Carl Andre and Richard Serra.

Non-Western Art
Almost all art traditions outside the European-American continuum are included in the non-Western art section. Although Dallas Museum of Art collections include Classical, ancient Mediterranean and Near Eastern, and Oriental Art, the major focus of the Museum's third level is devoted to pre-Columbian art (America before European arrival) and the so-called primitive art traditions of Africa, Oceania (the Pacific islands), Indonesia, and the American Indians.

In the pre-Columbian art of Middle America (Mexico and upper Central America), Central America, and South America, the Dallas holdings form one of the principal North American collections. Special strengths are found in the early art traditions of the Olmec of Mexico and the Chavin of Peru. The gold collection — representing the ancient peoples of Panama, Colombia, and Peru — is also exceptional. It is a part of the Nora and John Wise Collection of approximately 2,700 pieces, which also is rich in ceramics and textiles.

Almost equally important nationally is the African collection, comprised primarily of the almost 250 piece Clark and Frances Stillman Collection of Congo Sculpture and the fifty-plus piece Gustave and Franyo Schindler Collection of African Sculpture. Qualitatively this collection is exceptional, and has the greatest depth of representation of Congolese art found in any public collection in the United States.

Oceanic, Indonesian, and American Indian holdings are relatively few in number, but maintain a high qualitative level. They include a number of 19th century examples from New Ireland and the Eskimo. For the first several years in the new museum the Indonesian area will include an exceptional group of 52 pieces loaned by the Barbier-Muller Museum of Geneva, Switzerland. This loan makes the Indonesian area the best representation of indigenous Indonesian art in the New World.

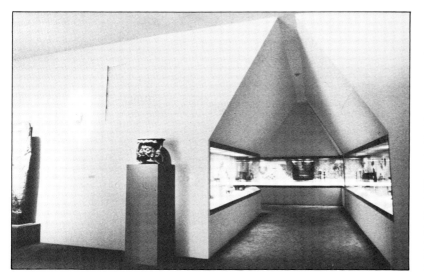

Entrance into Peruvian Gold Gallery, Dallas Museum of Art.

As a totality, the pre-Columbian and primitive holdings of the Dallas Museum of Art are of major national importance. Their number and quality are unusual in an art museum. They thus form one of the distinctive differences of the Dallas Museum of Art.

Collection Development Plan

The scope of the Museum's collections is more a product of chance and donor preference than truly the result of a master plan. As a civic museum in a community with numerous private collectors, it may be anticipated that the growth of the collection will continue to reflect the enthusiasm and generosity of collectors who give their collections to the public. Increasingly, however, Dallas aspires to raising sufficient acquisition funds to plan the collection according to priorities set by professional staff and trustees. A formal collection development plan has been shaped by judgment of opportunity and need. Building a collection of quality in the

last years of the twentieth century is going to be difficult, competitive, and expensive, but Dallas is resolved to play in the biggest leagues. The key to this effort is judged to be raising of acquisition endowment funds of at least $60 million. A campaign to raise this amount is already underway with the public portion planned for next year. A substantial recent boost has been generated by the gift of the Wendy and Emery Reves collection of Impressionist paintings and European decorative arts. The gift of this single collection doubles the value of the Museum's permanent collection and adds a whole new area of collection, the decorative arts, which is largely ignored by other museums in our region.

Education Wing

One of the most innovative features of the new Museum is an entire wing devoted to education programming. As visitors enter the Gateway Gallery from the main corridor, they are greeted by a variety of participatory activities, including a texture tunnel and mirror house. The Education Wing has been christened the "Gateway Gallery" to indicate that it is a gateway to understanding art and the Museum's permanent collection. The programmes and facilities are designed so that the young and the young at heart can learn about art in an exciting and innovative way.

This space of 8,500 square feet boasts orientation areas, an education exhibit, a library resource room, and two large studios. Visitors can learn about the permanent collection and temporary exhibitions from elaborate slide presentations programmed by Dr. Anne Bromberg, Curator of Education, which are shown in the orientation auditorium. School groups enter the Dallas Museum of Art through a courtyard designed

Gateway Gallery Exhibition – The Art Elements. Dallas Museum of Art.

St. Paul Street Entrance,
Dallas Museum of Art.

by artist Richard Fleischner. Once inside the building, docents can refer to a Time Line and World Map created by Houston artist Jack Boynton and use the "Orientation Well" before taking a group on its tour.

The orientation well has a special feature for all visitors, a video art box, which offers a variety of short didactic and creative video tapes.

The programmes in the two large art studios contain "Discovery Boxes" which each contain a self-directed art activity. Eleven boxes have been completed on such topics as sculpture, clay, mixing paints, mobiles, mood, spinning colours, texture, artist's viewpoint, weaving, Africa and archeology.

Programmed events include artists' demonstrations and directed art activities on Saturday and Sunday afternoons. The Museum continues to offer workshops and special classes, including visits to the galleries, gallery activities, and studio projects. The special classes are offered on a variety of topics for both children and adults. These provide a more in-depth look at cultures represented in the collection or aspects of art.

Education Courtyard
Artist Richard Fleischner has created a site-specific work for the Education Courtyard. His project was selected through an invitation competition with the criteria that the Courtyard both function effectively for Education Department programmes and be visually integrated into the Museum's architecture. His installation is composed of Indiana limestone placed in a series of step and planar elements. It is used for activities ranging from drawing classes to dramatic presentations for both children and adults.

"Cafe Terrace at Night" –
Vincent Van Gogh, Dallas
Museum of Art.

Sculpture Garden

The 1.2 acre Sculpture Garden, designed by Museum architect Edward Larrabee Barnes with landscape created by Dan Kiley, features four limestone water walls which flow into a series of canals which divide the Garden into six "galleries". The Garden also contains a reflecting pool that faces the windows of the contemporary galleries. Sixty live oak trees and jasmine groundcover have been planted throughtout the Garden, and the gate is framed with a wisteria-covered trellis.

The Sculpture Garden also serves as the setting for a series of public programmes designed to introduce the Sculpture Garden to downtown neighbours and the general public. The Education Department has created a programme of performance and educational events, which include special lunchtime programmes on Wednesdays and Sundays, ranging from music to creative sailboat construction. Artist demonstrations and special classes are also held and docents give tours of the Garden.

Budget and Operations

The site and physical facility (and, until recently, the collection) of the Dallas Museum of Art belonged to the City of Dallas and are funded — quite generously — on an annual operating basis (currently 11.8% of the cost including all utilities). However, the funding level is quite flat and the percentage of support funded by the private sector must be continually expanded. The primary engine of programme growth has been increased membership income, currently 26,000 members contributing a total of $3,000,000 per year. Considerable staff energy goes into the servicing of members with programmes and special social events as well as previews of exhibitions, discounts in the restaurant, a monthly calendar, and quarterly bulletins.

Sculpture Garden, Dallas Museum of Art.

Profit Centres

American art museums have developed the earned income sector in a sophisticated way largely borrowed from commerce. The shop, restaurant, parking and special event activities are budgeted as "profit centres" meaning that the museum runs them as businesses with the clearly perceived purpose of generating a profit to underwrite the activities and services of the museum. Such activities can be quite profitable. In 1984-85 Dallas earned $1,400,000 and generated a profit of $180,000 from shop, restaurant, and special events. The "special events" centre is the most profitable area with off-hour receptions, dinners, and other events sponsored by corporations and other organizations. Businesses pay to be eligible to hold such events as well as pay per capita fees for the overheads associated with the event. The Museum has its own license to sell drinks to the party hosts and often provides hors d'œuvres and meals through its restaurant staff. The activity is lucrative and also serves public relations purposes by attracting to the museum many Dallas visitors who would not otherwise come. Clear guidelines exist for the use of Museum space to protect the collection and facility, and a staff member is hired full-time to schedule and administer these special events.

Modern Management Techniques

More than our European counterparts, American museums have developed entrepreneurial skills borrowed from the "for profit" sector. These practices include extensive use of public opinion surveys, consumer research, and marketing practices. Determining demographics and preferences has become a quite exact science with a thorough visitor survey indicating the nature of the total visiting attendance. Modes of transportation, methods of communication, and patterns of use can be determined with certainty, and through computer analysis, easily sorted to compare weekend versus weekday audiences, members versus non-members, or local visitors versus out-of-town visitors. Perhaps most important is the philosophical attitude which gives priority to responsiveness to the consumer. Convenience of scheduling, relevance of activities, sufficiency of information – such issues can be subjected to quantitative testing and evaluation and user input. Of course, the museum retains its responsibility to be creative in generating services and modes of presentation which in turn are improved and polished through response analysis.

Planning and Staffing

In the last decade, almost all American art museums have seen the advantages of thoughtful and substantive long-range planning. Defining goals is surely a traditional obligation, but the development of formally adopted and detailed long-range plans is rather new. Usually, trustees and staff work together to set the plan, often with advice from professional planning consultants. The ambitions of the institution are defined, price tags established, and time schedules and staff responsibilities assigned. Often such plans become the basis of fund-raising "case" presentations to the community. The main purpose of such efforts is to establish a generally-approved thrust for the institution which has received the blessing of all who are to be involved – including those who will be asked to fund the effort. The practice of including non-professionals, principally the Board of Trustees, but also other interested people in the community, in helping to establish the future programme gives American art museums their particular dynamism and sense of momentum.

Staffing of the art museum has changed dramatically in recent years. While the curator is still the dominant professional title, he or she is now joined by a wide range of professionals, most of whom are recruited outside the art history background. This would include comptrollers, public relations officers, fund-raisers, as well as the librarians, registrars, and educators who have traditionally been allied to the curator in museum work. Personnel in these areas must normally be recruited outside the traditional networks and often require the services of specialized "head hunters" with access to candidates in non-museum specialties. Once assembled, their work must be blended with curatorial authorities in a team approach which tends to downplay the historic personal charismatic and creative role of the Director, who now tends to become a Chief Executive Officer in the corporate sense co-ordinating and bringing forth diverse individual contributions. Leadership today requires more participation by staff, better perceived objectives, and overall, a sense of balance and calm. Such qualities are somewhat distant from the personality cults of yesteryear, although leadership styles remain diverse.

Public/Private Funding Balance

Fundamental to the Dallas Museum of Art's prosperity is a balance of funding sources. We do receive substantial City funding but also federal, state, and education district funding. Foundations and corporations are substantial annual donors (corporate membership is 23% of the total membership income) with additional grants for special purposes such as exhibitions and programmes amounting to an additional $175,000. Individual contributions and memberships are the Dallas Museum's most significant sources of funds (44%), although this is exceptionally high among American art museums, most of whom rely more heavily upon endowment fund income. The income from the endowment of the Dallas Museum of Art is only 5%. Auxiliary activities account for 21% of the total income and 18% of the expense, making an annual contribution in profit of $180,000 towards the Museum's operating budget.

Relevance of the American Experience

The specifics of our management, funding, and collection development plans are quite different from what I imagine to be the local conditions in Scotland. I confess to ignorance of your particular mechanisms, although over the past three weeks, I have seen first-hand the remarkable collections of your National Gallery and Kelvingrove, the remarkable Burrell Collection, and the uniqueness of The Hermitage — to mention just a few examples of quality to which we in Dallas earnestly aspire. There is a sense of forward motion, of momentum and self-improvement, to American museums which does strike me as more dynamic than any other country. I attribute this momentum to generous funding, but also to will and imagination, to planning and clear thinking. Perhaps most of all, I attribute the current exceptional progress to a broad sense of participation by the public, and especially by those exceptional non-professional citizens who have become involved with the institutions as members of their Boards. Harnessing the energy of the community has been our special secret of success.

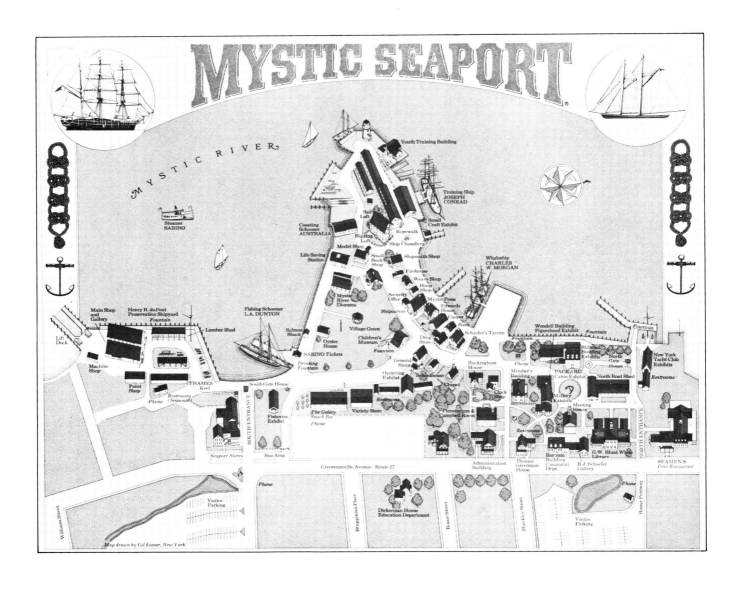

MYSTIC SEAPORT

*Mystic Seaport Map gives
visitors a sense of the scope
of the museum and a guide
to exhibit areas.*

Education Everywhere for Everyone at Mystic Seaport

J. Revell Carr

The Director of Mystic Seaport Museum, J. Revell Carr received degrees from Rutgers University and the University of Pennsylvania. After joining the Seaport staff in the Education Department in 1969, he assumed responsibilities as its Chief Curator in 1970 and as its Director in 1978.

Mr. Carr has served as President of the Council of American Maritime Museums, is currently President of the International Congress of Maritime Museums, is a Trustee of the National Trust for Historic Preservation and was Chairman of the Maritime Heritage Task Force of the National Trust.

Mystic Seaport has evolved and developed into an extensive museum complex over the years, and annually welcomes nearly a half-a-million visitors. It was not, however, originally conceived in its present form and the museum, with its strong emphasis on education, has been one that has grown and changed as it sought new ways to bring our American and overseas visitors closer to our maritime heritage. We are still planning, growing, and changing as we develop new initiatives in this field and seek to serve a broader audience more effectively. I will attempt to briefly outline for you the exceptional scope of the educational effort at Mystic Seaport, looking primarily at what we are doing today in two educational approaches. The first might be termed traditional education, and the second is what I might call education for the unsuspecting, that innocent visitor for whom education is the last thing on his mind. I will also comment briefly on what lies ahead for the museum, but feel that it is appropriate to give a brief historical survey on the institution to set it into perspective.

As American museums, and particularly outdoor museums, are concerned, Mystic is what I would term a mature institution. Since its founding, its evolution has been an outgrowth of what creative minds at the museum have perceived as the needs of the visitor, balanced by the research and preservation efforts. In the late 1920s, three residents of the Connecticut shipbuilding town of Mystic, located on the southern coast of New England, realized that the evidence of the maritime activities of this community was being lost at an alarming rate. Ship's logbooks and documents were rotting in attics or being thrown away, and the builders' half-models, which were in fact the designs for ships built in the community's eight shipyards, were so plentiful they were being burned for firewood. The perception of these three individuals brought the museum into existence on Christmas Day of 1929, which, on the heels of the Wall Street stock market crash, seemed like an unusual time to start a new venture. Somehow, the infant preservation institution stayed alive, and as it grew, it attracted the attention of some very prominent individuals who were active in the American shipping and yachting fields, and who began to support the institution. The idea that this could be more than a traditional museum with four walls and stuffy static galleries was born during the thirties, and by the end of that decade the museum, which had been collecting small boats from its earliest days, was looking for larger ships to rescue.

The opportunity occurred in 1941, when the museum took on the last of the American wooden whaleships, the CHARLES W.

The 1841 whaleship CHARLES W. MORGAN, the only ship of her kind in the world, gives visitors a unique experience.

MORGAN, at age 100. After the war, the energies of the small staff and active Trustees were channelled towards physical and academic growth. On the empty peninsula that had been the site of a 19th-century shipyard where clippers, including a record-setting DAVID CROCKETT, were built, historic maritime buildings threatened in other locations found sanctuary. The elements of a 19th-century maritime community were brought together, while on another aspect of the site more traditional formal museum galleries displayed the art and artifacts relating to our story. In 1947, the ship JOSEPH CONRAD, which had been built as a Danish training vessel in 1883, and which Alan Villiers had sailed around the world, was presented to the museum by the federal government, and within two years, the Education Department, which had been founded in 1946, began our Youth Training Programme aboard the JOSEPH CONRAD. In the decades that followed, more buildings were acquired, and more programmes developed. In 1954, the museum began the first of its university-level programmes. Today, on the 40-acre site, more than 60 buildings constitute the museum complex, which includes the historic village area, the formal exhibits, the only ship preservation shipyard in the world, and numerous other museum functions. Also included is a late-19th-century New England factory building containing 150,000 square feet of space which is viewed as the museum's primary growth opportunity in the decade ahead.

The museum, then, is large physically and, like any museum, it has as its primary role the preservation of historical objects. For us, however, these objects only have meaning when they are made available to the public, and it is in this effort that we broadly define

In the setting of the early 1800s, visitors observe and participate in the fireplace cooking demonstration.

our educational role. Our Statement of Purpose begins with a broad and rather idealistic statement, but then goes on to specifically cite responsibilities the museum has, and the first among these is to education. The opening statement reads, "The purpose of Mystic Seaport Museum is to preserve materials, artifacts, vessels, and skills relating to maritime history in order to enhance man's knowledge and understanding of the sea's influence on American life". The statement then goes on to say, "The staff, Trustees, and members have these major responsibilities: they must *educate the public* by an accurate presentation and interpretation of America's maritime past". It then goes on to talk about preservation of artifacts, perpetuation of skills, refinement of the collection, etc., but the point is, we have recognized that the education element is the essential issue that

permeates the entire museum. It is appropriate to look first at the offerings that the museum has for those who are seeking education. These might be termed traditional educational programmes in that they involve instructors and students, but even in these programmes, there is a sense of the unconventional and untraditional.

There is, of course, the typical day visit of a school group to the museum. While we would like to work closely with every group that comes, this is not always possible because of the sheer volume of visits at certain times of year, and because of the desire of the teacher to have a less structured visit to the museum. In any instance, the group receives pre-visit material which helps to orient them to the aspects of the museum that relate to their level of study, and, in order to ensure that the museum is not overrun by students who therefore have a diminished experience, we take the drastic step of limiting student reservations to 1,000 young people per day during the spring weeks.

For the museum teachers on the staff, a far more appealing school group programme is one in which groups come and stay one or two nights at the museum, living aboard one of our ships. In this way, the students have sufficient time to immerse themselves in the museum. The staff museum teachers have an opportunity to work with them over the period of two days, including evening presentations, so that their understanding of aspects of American maritime history is developed in some detail. The museum staff works with the classroom teacher to integrate the museum presentation with their area of study. Recently, the museum staff completed the development of a grade school curriculum for maritime study which has now been published and is available to the classroom teachers. With this type of in-depth work, and with the ability to house up to 60 youngsters at a time, the Seaport has an unusual offering which can be equalled by very few museums in our country.

The JOSEPH CONRAD's primary use remains in the field of sail training, the purpose for which this ship was originally built. However, the CONRAD herself no longer goes to sea. She remains in the museum as an artifact which can be visited by the public, and where they can experience first-hand the orderly mass of lines required to create a full ship's rig. On board during the summer months, youngsters will be in residence for week-long programmes which teach sailing in small boats on the river, as well as the fundamentals of piloting, dead reckoning, and basic navigation. Obviously, during their week-long stay, the students in the Youth Training Programme are exposed to the other exhibits and programmes of the museum. This programme is now in its 36th year.

The museum is fortunate to be able to offer to both young people and adults the opportunity for an off-shore educational experience through our half-century-old schooner yacht, BRILLIANT. Until recently, this vessel worked exclusively with young people as a second level of training for those who had already completed the programme aboard the JOSEPH CONRAD. However, in recent years, it has been realized that there are a great many adults who have a sufficiently serious interest in sailing aboard a yacht of the calibre of BRILLIANT to develop a special programme for them. This summer, in order to provide this experience, BRILLIANT made the passage to and from Bermuda with adult crews. Whether it is with

young people or adults, the training aboard BRILLIANT is thorough and adheres to the highest standards. The master of this schooner is an American who studied in Great Britain and for five years was the headmaster of a school here.

Shifting now from programmes which are aimed at school-age youngsters or Sail Training, we should focus on what are perhaps the most traditional educational programmes within the museum. For over 30 years the museum, under the auspices of its Munson Institute, has conducted graduate-level courses during the summer months, with credit given by several universities in the state of Connecticut. Courses in maritime history and literature are regularly offered, as well as an independent study offering. This course has been attended by graduate students as well as secondary school teachers who have then carried the maritime studies curriculum back to their own classrooms. It has also been a course that has been attended by many staff members of Mystic Seaport and other American maritime museums, and has filled gaps in their training. It is gratifying to see the number of graduates of this programme who are active in the field today.

With an awareness of the positive benefits from the graduate-level programme, a group working on a long-range plan for the museum twelve years ago realized that there was an obvious lack of opportunity for maritime study at the undergraduate college level in the United States. Eight years ago, the museum, in partnership with Williams College, a fine, small liberal-arts college in our region, established an undergraduate programme, taught entirely at the museum, in which 21 students each term come from 17 participating colleges and pursue their

Stoic sentinels, the figureheads that once adorned the bows of great ships create a dramatic impression in their exhibit.

studies at the museum. While in residence at the Seaport, the students take courses in maritime history, maritime literature, marine science, and a seminar focusing on sea policy, looking at issues such as law of the sea, offshore oil drilling, sea bed mining, and others. As part of this course, students go to sea on a sailing research vessel for two weeks of their term.

Museum studies is not a part of the curriculum for either of our college-level programmes. However, there is a real interest in pursuing this area of study. To meet that desire, the museum developed an intern programme which is offered during the summer months. No fee is charged for the programme, and the museum exchanges training for work done by the interns, so that everyone benefits. A typical five-day week for the interns includes two days of training sessions with a number of museum staff members, two days of work within a museum department, and one day consisting of a field trip to another institution in our region for

comparison. This informal internship has proven to be both popular and beneficial, not only to those seeking to enter the museum profession, but to some already involved in small institutions who wish to improve their knowledge and skills.

One of the largest elements of our traditional education offerings is what might be generally termed "adult education." Throughout the United States there are increasing opportunities for those who have already completed their formal education to pursue other topics for their edification and enjoyment. The Seaport has realized it is in an unusual position to be able to meet the needs and interests of many individuals. Among the maritime skills offered, for example, is Celestial Navigation, which is taught to yachtsmen through the museum's Planetarium. For others, there is an interest in learning to sail or in refining their sailing skills and racing tactics, and these are taught in adult sailing classes, which are held on both weekdays and weekends in the spring and fall. For those with an even more basic interest, avocational boat-building has been one of the most successful offerings for well over a decade. When the boat-building courses began, they were offered as evening programmes, with an individual attending a two-hour class one night a week for ten weeks. Due to the demand, classes were given five nights a week. We realized that, in order to obtain this instruction, some people were travelling more than 175 miles each way one night a week to attend these classes. Out of a concern for the safety of these people commuting in winter months over such long distances, we developed a concentrated three-day weekend boat-building course which has attracted students from across the continent. Among the maritime skills offered ashore, the museum has conducted courses in wood-carving in the tradition of the ship-carver of past centuries. A few years ago, the United States experienced a fuel shortage which had an impact on the museum's income. Our young shipsmith, in an effort to be productive during the quiet winter months, suggested that, since she neither had a great deal of ironwork to turn out for the museum nor did she have a great number of visitors to whom to interpret her craft, perhaps someone would be interested in taking shipsmith classes. She was indeed correct, and her hours were filled teaching in her new classes, which produced income and helped to offset the income shortfall.

In a more domestic area, the museum for many years has conducted classes in weaving and, during the fuel crisis, realized that there was another area in which Americans could economize. As a regular part of the museum's interpretive demonstrations, fireplace cooking is carried out. Since many Americans were using their fireplace to supplement their heating, a number were interested in using that heat to prepare their food, and fireplace cooking classes became very successful.

In recent years five annual symposia have been developed which are related to the museum's research interests, and which clearly have found a responsive segment of the population. Each autumn, a maritime history symposium is conducted, with its primary focus being the maritime history of southern New England. In the spring, a similar symposium focuses on life during the Victorian era in America, since this represents the time period of our village exhibit area. In early summer, a sea music symposium and festival serves well to both encourage a serious academic approach to the music of the sea while at the same time providing a most entertaining weekend for visitors to the museum. Another segment of the population is interested in collecting antiques, and we felt we could serve effectively in teaching these individuals how to care for the objects in their collections. These conservation symposia have been very well received. Our small craft workshop each year attracts several hundred small boat enthusiasts who come to study, attend lectures, and exchange information on the collecting and preserving of traditional small boats.

Through all of these programmes, the Seaport is reaching segments of the population and passing on to them information in their specific areas of interest. The museum does not feel constrained to restrict its effort to these topics, and if interest wanes in any of these, there are new offerings being constantly developed.

We often look at the traditional sorts of instructional programmes as the museum's educational effort, but, at Mystic, it is far wider. Areas such as the documentation and publication efforts of the museum play an enormous educational role. Throughout the museum a variety of documentation programmes are carried out simply as good museum practice. However, this information must be made available, either to researchers actually visiting the museum or to a broader public when possible. Like many museums, we periodically make oral or videotapes of individuals or maritime activities for the purpose of recording them before they are lost in history. In other projects, interesting data has been gathered through the use of x-rays of figureheads in the museum's collection. Through these images, construction and fascinating details can be observed, as can earlier repair and restoration, without harming the figurehead, and this data is available to interested researchers.

In documenting the work that goes on in ship restoration at the museum, a combination of recording techniques is employed. Written narratives describe the work that has gone on, and these are supplemented by several types of visual images. Still photographs are used to record certain aspects of a project: film or videotape records are made if appropriate; and traditional naval architects' drawings are prepared showing what areas and elements of the ship have been restored. In an effort to record much of the hidden, complex, detailed construction, our staff has developed a drawing technique which is able to delineate the complex construction that will be hidden once restoration is complete.

The museum, then, distributes this material in two ways: the first and most obvious is through our printed materials. Members of the museum are kept aware of the projects and activities of the museum through the newsletter, *Wind Rose*, and are offered a broader look at maritime history through the museum's quarterly, *The Log*. In addition to these two publications going to our members, the museum has three publication programmes. The first is a publication series issued by the museum known as *The American Maritime Library*, and through this effort, important books in the American maritime field have been published. In addition, under the museum's name, a variety of books and monographs have been published in recent years. Another area of publication which is attracting greater interest is that of ship and boat plans, with more than 1,200 sets of plans sold each year. The museum has an exceptional collection in this area, and over the years we have seen a steady increase in the interest in ships' plans. Through these plans, and all of our other printed materials, the museum's educational effort reaches out beyond the physical confines of the museum itself, and beyond this generation, preserving and making available this information for those of future generations.

With the emphasis in society today, particularly in the United States, on video technology, the entire area of film and video recording and distribution has taken on increased importance. We have been acquiring historic film footage for many years, and now have virtually hundreds of hours of documentary footage in the museum's collection. In addition, we have made our own film and video recordings of ship restoration, boat-building, and other projects around the museum. We know that the use of film or video recordings can be an effective way to reach a potentially vast audience. In our preliminary offerings, the museum has prepared a number of videotape cassettes from historic footage and has offered these cassettes for sale for use on home video players. The response has been fast and encouraging, and it would appear that, with additional material being available, the museum will sell more than $200,000 worth of home video cassettes during the next year.

We are also examining the use of other video technology, not only for the recording of images, but their distribution as well. The museum recently acquired a phenomenal photographic collection containing one million images covering one hundred years of the American maritime story. As we contemplate the cataloguing of this collection, the use of video disks becomes a key element in the process. With each twelve-inch disk capable of containing 56,000 images which can be called up at random, the potential is enormous for distributing this photographic collection around the world on a series of disks, or the segmenting of the collection and publishing the core elements of it, and the sale of those disks to libraries, other museums, or individuals if they desired it.

We need to explore this area even further, to see if the video technology is suitable for other publishing endeavours. Recently the museum published a conventional book on its figurehead collection. This topic might well have adapted beautifully to a video publishing format, with the video camera able to move all around the figurehead, focusing on details as the narrator both presented the information about that specific figurehead and described the details. One of the joys of video publishing, of course, is that the cassettes can be produced on demand, and funds are not tied up in stock. To properly realize the full benefit of this aspect of the

museum's educational effort, the Seaport has had to develop methods for outreach and distribution. We are in the beginning stages of work with the National Geographic Society that will provide for the production of video programmes for transmission through the cable television system, and can therefore carry the museum into virtually millions of homes. Certainly it is desirable to have people encounter the real object in the museum environment, but the use of video broadcast provides enormous outreach and hopefully will then encourage viewers to visit the museum and see the actual objects. Certainly for both the conventional printed material and the video and film material that is available for rent or sale, the distribution system and dealer network is essential in getting information out to the potential audience, and our museum continues to broaden its distribution network.

It should be mentioned here that the programmes of the not-for-profit museum are complemented by the Museum Store, which is a wholly-owned, profit-making subsidiary corporation of our museum. Through two aspects in particular, the store is helping to carry out the museum's educational role. Its book department has developed into the finest maritime book store in our region, if not the nation, and through a free telephone number, people around the country can call and order the maritime publications which are very difficult or impossible to obtain from their local book dealers. Clearly, the bookstore is providing an important educational service. Likewise, the store's Gallery focuses on contemporary marine art, and encourages artists to work in this field while at the same time providing good, contemporary paintings, sculpture, ship models and scrimshaw for collectors. Through this Gallery the museum

Visitors encounter "Mrs. Ashby", a role-playing interpreter who describes life in the 1880's as they talk outside the General Store.

feared as connoting what many Frenchmen automatically think of when the word museum is mentioned. As Daniel Charles wrote, "The real name of the spot is Mystic Seaport Museum. That last word will freeze those who wandered into one of our hexagonal museums, official repositories of a dusty naval culture."

We are what might be described as a popular museum. With our outdoor atmosphere and our variety of exhibition offerings, we are less intimidating than some great monolithic museum structures, and most people approach the museum with the primary thought of having a good time and the secondary thought of it being an interesting (and therefore educational) time. Even with our name, we have the ability to downplay the word "museum" as many of our outdoor sister institutions do. Most of the outdoor museums in the States, such as Colonial Williamsburg, Old Sturbridge Village, and Greenfield Village do not use the word "museum" in their titles. In many instances, we simply drop the word museum and refer to ourselves, or are referred to, as Mystic Seaport, and this does not bother me a bit. Whether we use the word museum or not in our title does not affect the quality of the programmes or the integrity of our educational effort, and if it makes a travelling family more relaxed in their approach to the institution, and therefore more receptive to our message, all the better.

Dealing with a group of visitors as large and varied as ours creates some difficulties as how best to label and interpret, and at what level to aim our presentations. A number of years ago I had my consciousness raised on this issue abruptly one day when a visitor from the central section of the country asked,

is able to continually show the work of contemporary artists in a venue where it can be for sale, rather than in the conventional gallery within the museum, where we would not have paintings for sale. One segment of the Gallery's work is the publication of fine maritime graphics, and, again, there is an outreach from the museum that serves another constituency.

We have looked, now, at some of the ways in which the museum responds to those who are coming to it seeking education through courses, classes, and publications. But what about all of those others — the hundreds of thousands of people each year who become the unsuspecting victims of our educational thrust? It is with these people that I believe Mystic Seaport is most effective, and for whom our staff is most creative. A recent article in the French sailing magazine, *Neptune*, featured Mystic Seaport Museum and cautioned its readers that, in the case of Mystic Seaport, the word "museum" was not to be in all seriousness, "What are the large white birds?" They were, of course, seagulls, and it had never occurred to me that there would be people visiting the museum who had never seen them. Of course, now the seagulls have difficulty flying with the large labels we have hung on them, but it is all in the interest of education! We also have to think, because of this variety in our visitors, of even the most subtle experiences. While here in the U.K. you have such a rich historical tradition and have preserved so many of your ancient monuments, we have either succeeded in tearing them down or covering them up in so many instances that older elements of our culture are difficult to find in some areas. Of course, some areas of the country were not settled and developed until well into the 19th-century, so, for example, there are people coming to the museum who have never experienced the joys of wobbling down a cobblestone street in high-heeled shoes. That, and many other subtle elements of the

Skilled craftsmen build elegant small boats in the boat-building shop while other craftsmen apply their talents to ship restoration.

museum's environment, are all part of the education we offer.

All of us here know that the interpretation of our collections is of utmost importance in properly conveying our message to our visitors. We essentially use three basic forms of interpretation: live interpretation through paid staff members; printed labels; and audiovisual techniques, with the emphasis essentially in that order.

We firmly believe that good, live interpretation is the most effective in our kind of museum, but naturally we are continually aware of the expense involved in this approach. However, our visitors need the interactive quality of this kind of interpretation in which they meet and talk with knowledgeable staff members who can respond to their specific questions about an exhibit.

Within the interpretation division of our Education Department there are five basic types of live interpretation. The first involves the interpretation within our formal exhibits. In this instance, the interpreter serves as a supplement to the printed label used predominantly in this sort of exhibit. At certain times, in some of the galleries, the interpreters give formal gallery talks, but more often they attempt to work with the visitor, supplying information as needed to enhance the visitor's experience in that particular exhibit.

Within our historic buildings in the village area, there are a variety of crafts, trades, and lifestyles to be interpreted for the visitor. It has not been possible for the museum to have live interpretation in every one of these structures, so that graphic interpretive presentations are used in some of these buildings. The emphasis has been to use live interpreters in the exhibits where there is a process to be explained or where a broad segment of 19th-century life can be interpreted. Within the shops, such as the General Store, the Drugstore, or the Ship Chandlery, the interpreters not only explain specific items within their exhibit, but also relate the role of their particular shop or business to the major theme of life ashore. The houses also follow this same approach, and in one of them the fireplace cooking demonstration uses produce from the house garden and fish that is split and dried, or smoked in our smokehouse, as part of other museum demonstrations.

Where there is a process to be interpreted, in some instances the visitor will find an actual craftsman at work, and in others a demonstration of the process and how the tools are used, but not an actual production operation. In the Shipsmith Shop, ironwork for the museum's vessels is produced. In the Navigational Instrument Shop, instruments and clocks are restored and repaired, and in our Cooperage, the barrel-making process and the tools used in that trade are described. The Boat-Building Shop is an exception to the conventional village interpretation. It does not purport to be a 19th-century shop, and in fact has 20th-century power tools. The bulk of the work, however, on the delicate boats that are built here is carried out by hand with traditional tools. The boats are sold and the income helps to offset the cost of this demonstration, which we feel is particularly relevant to our museum, so that the visitor can actually see vessel construction taking place at all times. During the busy visitor months, an interpreter is stationed in the boat shop to answer questions and explain the process, while the boat-builders continue at

their work, stopping only to respond to the particularly complex question when appropriate.

With so many maritime activities being ones that would normally take place outside, we maintain a group of young interpreters whose assignment is to carry out these activities throughout the day. At certain times they will be in the rigging of our tall ships, setting or furling sails, with the visitors participating on deck under supervision. At other times, they may be demonstrating the use of a whaleboat, the making of fish nets, the use of oystering equipment, the traditional "Dead Horse" ceremony, or the rescue procedures using a breeches buoy. These demonstrations seem to be of particular interest to the visitors.

Another activity which is normally carried out outside is our music programme. The work songs and other music of the sea has a unique quality, and skilled musicians are continually playing and singing around the grounds while giving the historical background for their music.

Within the Seaport's Children's Museum, the theme is life at sea for children in the 19th-century, and outdoors during certain times of the year children are challenged to participate in 19th-century amusements such as stilt-walking and hoop-rolling.

The majority of the interpretive staff is not normally in costume. However, throughout the year, there are a few staff members on the grounds in accurate costumes, playing the roles of 19th-century characters. It may be a ship's captain or first mate, home from a voyage, or the captain's wife with a letter in her hand from her husband who is half a world away. These individuals interact with the visitors, yet only speak to them from the 19th-century, and will not come out of character. This can be extremely effective interpretation, but we feel it must be used in moderation, since it is intimidating and off-putting to some visitors. In a similar vein, there are costumed special events at various times of the year with larger numbers of staff in costume and greater visitor involvement. During the evenings at Christmas time, small groups of visitors are escorted through the museum from one location to another, where they will meet the characters from the 19th-century in homes, aboard ships, in the tavern, and in stores. As they progress chronologically through the century, not only do they have an enjoyable experience, but they learn the origins of the Christmas traditions in New England. Due to the limited time frame, this programme is restricted to approximately 4,000 people, and reservations sell out within the first days of their availability each year. Other special events and celebrations orientated toward national holidays create a lively atmosphere.

In the last fifteen years, great attention has been paid to the training of our interpretive staff, and because of this the quality of their presentations has continuously improved. It is natural for curricula to be developed for traditional academic courses, but the Education Department and staff has essentially developed a curriculum for each of the twenty interpreted exhibits, with the educational goals and objectives which interpreters are seeking to achieve. The personal skills of the interpreters are taxed in that they are not given a written speech to present, but rather are expected to present their material in an interesting and personalized manner, so that the visitor does

not find himself confronted with the same style of presentation at every exhibit.

Another method for the low-key transfer of information to our visitors is through presentations that are more shows than they are lectures. This does not affect the accuracy of the information presented, but these programmes are aimed at the general museum visitor. Presentations of this sort are made both in our Planetarium, where the focus is on celestial navigation, and in a presentation titled *Whales, Whaling, and Whalemen*, which supplements the other information the visitor receives on the subject of the American whaling industry, which was a very significant part of 19th-century New England maritime life.

Another extensively-utilized technique is the use of printed labels and interpretive graphics. Obviously a key consideration is to have them printed and mounted in a way which enables them to be easily read, but the greatest challenge is in the content. When the subject is complex, the key is to make the label as clear and concise as possible, and throughout the museum a constant issue is, to what level of knowledge and understanding should the labels be addressed? With the range of our visitors, from learned maritime historians to the American family on holiday, this element is particularly challenging.

Our response with the printed labels and graphics has been to attempt to provide information in various levels of thoroughness. Our exhibit entitled *New England and the Sea* is a good example of this technique, with each major segment of the exhibit having a large, brief introductory label silk-screened on the banner that is suspended overhead. When the exhibit is crowded, or when people want to move quickly through an exhibit, these can always be easily read, and they give the visitor a basic understanding of the exhibit and its themes. At the next level there are a series of labels dealing with more detailed topics, each approximately 300 words in length. Finally, the exhibit cases and railings contain individual identification labels for each of the items on display. This technique, and variations on it, has proven effective in allowing the visitors to choose the amount of information they want on a specific topic.

Mystic Seaport does not draw heavily on audio-visual technology for its interpretation. This has been a deliberate decision, but it is probable that we will gradually increase our activity in this area.

In an even more subtle way, the opportunity for learning is available throughout the museum. This might be termed, if necessary, experiental learning, as the senses absorb information that otherwise is not extensively interpreted. Certainly aboard the museum's coal-fired passenger-carrying steamboat, SABINO, the last of its kind in America, there is interpretation about the boat and its propulsion system, but for the majority of the passengers who have grown up in the age of the internal combustion engine, with its explosions and noise, experiencing the gentle hissing of this boat's steam engine is indeed an education. Around the museum, other textures, visions, sounds, and smells are new to the visitor and enhance the experience. In addition to the cobblestones which I have already mentioned, there are road surfaces of dirt, Belgian block, crushed oyster shell, and macadam, some of which are textures which the visitor has never experienced underfoot. That unique smell of Stockholm tar used as a preservative on hemp and marlin pervades

the Ship Chandlery, while smoke from a coal stove contrasts with the hickory smoke that wafts out of the museum's smokehouse. Certainly, being downwind from the flakes where fish are drying in the sun is an unforgettable experience, and the sheer beauty that visitors encounter, whether it is in the form of figureheads, the graceful shape of a delicate small boat, or the elegance and harmony of the main salon of a ship from the 1880s attunes the eye to the beauties that resulted from a pre-mass-production, plastic, high-tech era. The sounds of the steamboat's whistle, or a concertina, or the life-saving cart's iron-bound wheels rumbling over cobblestones, are seldom experienced in other locations, and of course in the wintry months there is the joy and gratification of being able to gather near a pot-bellied stove glowing with heat. Throughout the museum, this subliminal learning touches every visitor.

I might comment at this point that Mystic Seaport, because of all the sights and sounds and smells and textures, can be a particularly positive experience for handicapped visitors. Certainly, unique problems are created for those on crutches or in wheelchairs, but the museum works hard to minimize barriers, and other aspects of our programmes and presentations prove particularly effective for those with mental, visual, or hearing impediments.

In contrast to what occurs in many museums, we have made an effort to move some aspects of our restoration and conservation out into the public view. The most dramatic aspect of this is within the museum's Preservation Shipyard. This facility has been developed to give visitor access to as many areas as possible, and, while there, they can observe the 35-man ship restoration crew at work,

The music of the sea rings out beneath the bow of the JOSEPH CONRAD as the Seaport's steamboat SABINO passes in the background.

sometimes with modern equipment, but always with traditional materials and, in many instances, traditional tools, meticulously restoring our ships or turning out masts on our 95-foot lathe.

Working on a different scale, the museum's model-builder and restorer works in the public area where his skills can be observed, which is also the case for clock and instrument repair in the Navigational Instrument Shop. In recent years, simply walking along the museum's waterfront has been an education

as the museum staff has been at work building 2,000 linear feet of permanent granite seawall.

I hope it is evident from these examples that the opportunity for learning is omnipresent within Mystic Seaport, but I should comment briefly on what makes this happen. While certainly money makes it happen, the commitment of many people is the key ingredient. The museum functions as a private, non-profit, tax-exempt educational institution. There is a Board of Trustees, the members of which volunteer their time to generally oversee the activity of the museum. A large paid staff, numbering more than 300 during the summer months, carries out the work around the museum, and they are supported by a volunteer corps, again numbering over 300 people, who annually contribute more than 25,000 hours of time. The museum is also supported by its 17,000 members from all areas of the United States and many other countries. In addition to these people who are directly involved, the hundreds of thousands of visitors each year help make the museum a success.

Addressing the financial situation briefly, the museum has a broad base of support. I should point out that it receives no ongoing, governmental operational support, but has had occasional government grants to assist with specific projects. The museum charges an admission fee that is in line with the fees charged by other outdoor museums in our country. This year we anticipate 440,000 visitors. The admission fees constitute approximately 40% of our income. Another 10% comes from tuitions and fees charged for programmes. Over the years the museum has developed an endowment fund, the interest from which is used to support operations, and the dues paid by our members aid considerably. As a non-profit organization, gifts and grants made to us by foundations, corporations, and individuals produce tax benefits for them and enable the donors to give more than they would normally. They are able to make direct contributions to the organization of their choice, rather than having the money processed through a government bureaucracy. The final, significant element in our income sources is from our auxiliary enterprises. Our food services do a volume of business nearing $2,500,000 per year, and our Museum Store and mail-order

business is a $4,000,000 annual operation. The income from these operations assists with the museum's budget, which is now nearing $8,000,000 a year, excluding the auxiliary enterprises.

I commented earlier that one of the strengths of the museum had been that it had changed and evolved, and this is a continuing process. I am positive about the future of our kind of museum, unconstrained by the traditions of four walls and gallery guards. In the future, we will be developing a new Watercraft Research Center, bringing together our boats, half-models, ships' plans, and boat-building instruction in one location that will become a visitor asset. We also realize that, during the 20th century, a great segment of the American population has been involved in yachting or pleasure boating, and we will be giving greater emphasis to the preservation of the history of this aspect of our maritime involvement. As I think we are all aware, the travelling public throughout the world has a fascination with food, and we are considering what more we can do in making traditional foods available at the museum. We also anticipate an expansion of our costuming programme when we are able to do this accurately and well, and will therefore be adding another interpretive element. Our future plan is extensive, although it focuses much more on refinement and improvement rather than growth. The museum will, however, continue to change.

I cannot pass up an opportunity such as this one to plead two of my deepest concerns. At a conference a few years ago, a representative of a commercial exhibit production firm told a group of maritime museum representatives that maritime museums had to find out what the public wanted and give it to them. To say I was disappointed is an understatement. That kind of visitor survey market study mentality, if broadly administered, would produce the same mediocrity within our museums that we have in so many of our magazines and in so much of our astonishing 20 channels of television. Certainly, we must talk with our visitors and, indeed, with those who have not visited the museum, to find out what works for them in visiting a museum, but as educators, it is our responsibility to determine what the curriculum should be, just as if we were a traditional school or college. Our visitors are coming to us to learn, and are not expected to know what they want. Once we have made that determination, then I think we use every bit of wit and creativity to make it as interesting, exciting, even entertaining, as it can be, all with the objective of helping them to absorb our information. If we simply ask them what they want and give it to them, we are abdicating our responsibility.

My other point is that we do not lose sight of the fact that we are museums. In this age of

Visitors gather along the waterfront to hear and see a demonstration of the use of a whaleboat and its equipment.

audio-visual wizardry and dramatic super-graphics, it is too easy to create a dazzling display and lose the essence of the museum, which is the preservation and interpretation of that object from the past. We must not lose "the real thing". When a person visits the Smithsonian Institution in Washington and sees George Washington's false teeth, an intimate moment has been created between George and that individual. Certainly when someone visits the National Maritime Museum in Greenwich, that most fascinating of objects, Lord Nelson's coat, transports them across more than a century and a half to the deck of VICTORY at Trafalgar. It is these objects, but it is the millions of other items and works of art that we care for, that we must use to help the people of today understand yesterday. Compromise should be avoided whenever possible, even in restoration. In Boston, on board the USS CONSTITUTION, which is cared for by our Navy, and in Portsmouth on board HMS VICTORY, black polypropylene line is being used in the rigging of these ships. I appreciate the problems of scale on which those preservation projects are operating, and the durability of the modern plastics, but at Mystic we are fortunate to be working with smaller vessels, and we also believe that continued care in the traditional manner is part of both our opportunity and our obligation to educate. When a young person goes aboard the CONSTITUTION or VICTORY and fingers the lanyards woven through deadeyes at the base of the rigging, their natural conclusion will be that black plastic rope was available to Isaac Hull aboard CONSTITUTION or Lord Nelson aboard VICTORY. At Mystic, however, they will find the real thing – natural hemp rope that has to be regularly tarred for its preservation – and, as they walk away with their sticky fingers, I hope they will understand a bit more about their past.

*The dining room of The
Newark Museum's
Ballantine House, showing
the Museum's rich holdings of
19th century decorative arts.*

The Role of Museum Management Training in Developing Effective Museum Managers

Andrea E. Glanz

Andrea E. Glanz was until recently Director of Continuing Professional Education at Museums Collaborative, a national museum service organization based in New York City. In this capacity, she was responsible for developing, marketing and managing conferences and seminars designed to strengthen the professional skills of senior level museum employees nationwide. Most notable among these is the Cultural Institutions Management Program, a series of seminars designed to improve the management capabilities of museum directors and other senior level personnel — the first programme of its kind in the United States.

This paper describes the Cultural Institutions Management Programme, an innovative training programme that has strengthened the management skills of senior museum professionals throughout the United States. By providing museum administrators with new management concepts and skills, the Programme has dramatically changed the way many American museums are managed.

Traditionally, and with rare exceptions, museum administrators have been educated in an academic discipline such as history, art history or the sciences. While this formal training has equipped them to work with museum collections, it has not prepared them to deal with the increasingly complex management issues that now confront them. Terms such as strategic planning, marketing and human resources management have only recently entered museum professionals' vocabularies. Yet museum administrators are responsible for managing sizable budgets and staffs, for safeguarding priceless collections, and for serving diverse and growing publics at a time when resources are scarce and mistakes are costly. Museums are the primary preservers of the world's cultural heritage, and many — including public and private funding agencies, museum audiences and museum professionals themselves — have come to feel that the management of these assets no longer can be left to instinct or chance.

In response to this need, in 1978 Museums Collaborative initiated the Cultural Institutions Management Programme, the first museum management training programme developed in the United States. The Programme is designed to improve the management skills of middle and executive level museum personnel and, through these individuals, to improve the management of cultural institutions.

The Programme was designed with the following goals in mind:
To provide participants with intensive exposure to management concepts and skills.
To provide experience in applying these concepts through group discussion and investigation of case studies designed to help participants analyse problems within their own institutions.
To provide a structure which ensures that these skills and concepts will be applied directly within participants' institutions.
To foster increased contact and sharing of management experience among participants by furnishing both formal and informal opportunities for interaction.

Lecturers for the Programme have been drawn from the Columbia University Graduate School of Business, the Harvard University Graduate School of Business Administration, and the J.L. Kellogg Graduate School of Management at Northwestern University. All have extensive backgrounds in not-for-profit management and years of experience in providing management education for executives. Through research and consultancies, as well as their involvement with the Cultural Institutions Management Programme, they have become highly attuned to the needs and operations of museums.

The Programme currently includes three courses. *Principles of Management for Cultural Institutions,* first offered in 1978, provides an intensive overview of general management topics including long-range strategic planning, financial management, marketing and human resources management. It is designed for those with broad managerial responsibilities. *Marketing for Audience and Income Development,* introduced in 1979, enables participants to define the marketing research needs of

their institutions, implement studies and interpret the resulting data. It is intended for Executive Directors and those involved with development, public relations, membership and education programmes.

Managing Human Resources for Organizational Effectiveness, added in 1980, is designed to strengthen participants' abilities in diagnosing and dealing with individual, group and organizational problems and in managing critical relationships with boards, colleagues and staffs. It is aimed at those for whom the management of human resources is a central responsibility.

All the courses use a unique learning model that combines the presentation of a formal curriculum with the requirement that participants execute individual projects that apply some aspect of the curriculum to problems or decisions faced by their institutions. The purpose of this approach is to guarantee that the concepts and skills presented in a theoretical context are actually translated into practice within each institution, thereby ensuring that the sponsoring institution directly benefits from a staff member's participation.

To achieve this, each course within the programme has three components:
An initial three- to six-day Institute, at a residential conference facility, in which a comprehensive management curriculum is presented.
A two- to three-month Practicum in which participants use the concepts and skills learned in the Institute to address a management problem within their own institutions. During this period, a one-day Interim Meeting is held, at which participants

"DINNER IN THE COUNTRY" can be arranged for a group of friends to enjoy an evening of cooking on the open hearth at Van Cortlandt Manor, one of the many offerings in the "Winter Workshops" programme sponsored by Sleepy Hollow Restorations.

institutional information-gathering tasks that must be completed before the programme begins. During the Institute, textbooks, articles and case studies are read as background to the topics presented. Instruction emphasizes the active involvement of participants, and employs such learning methods as case discussion, role playing, problem solving and small group activities, as well as lectures and class discussions.

Participants are expected to have significant management responsibility within their institutions. Generally speaking, they are Executive Directors or department heads. Additionally, they must have institutional endorsement. That is, if the applicant is a department head, the Executive Director of the institution must endorse the application; if the applicant is the Executive Director, the Chairman of the Board of Directors must sign the application. It is essential that a participant's supervisor understand the commitment of time (and sometimes funds) needed to carry out the Practicum project, and be willing to do everything in his or her power to facilitate its execution.

To assure personal attention and adequate group interaction, there are no more than 35 and no fewer than 20 participants enrolled in each course. To ensure the greatest benefit to the sponsoring institution and to the individual participant, the following factors are considered in the selection process:

The applicant's function and level of responsibility within the institution
The applicant's work history
The applicant's educational background
The applicant's personal statement of reasons for wishing to participate.

present written and oral progress reports, receive suggestions and recommendations from the faculty and their colleagues on the course, and define the tasks necessary for successful completion of the Practicum. A one- to three-day concluding Seminar in which participants present written and oral reports on their completed Practicum projects to the faculty and their peers.

Prior to each course, participants are given assignments including reading and

Since the Programme's inception, 281 individuals have participated in one or more courses, representing 218 museums located in 36 states, 4 Canadian provinces and the Commonwealth of Puerto Rico. In the *Principles of Management for Cultural Institutions* course, more than 50% of the participants have been Executive Directors of their institutions, with the remainder being divided between department heads and Deputy Directors in a two-to-one ratio. Budgets of the sponsoring museums have ranged from $10,000 to more than $75 million, with a median of $430,000. All types of museums have been represented, although art museums outnumber history or science museums by a ratio of approximately two-to-one.

The Cultural Institutions Management Programme has been evaluated formally by an external consultant as well as by participants through written comments submitted twice during each course. The evaluations repeatedly attest to the effectiveness of the learning model and to the significant impact that the courses have had on participants' institutions. That individuals often enroll in more than one course and enthusiastically recommend the programme to colleagues within their own institution as well as to those in other institutions, is further testimony to the value of the Programme in the eyes of participants.

Because cultural institutions are non-profit organizations with limited financial resources, the registration fees charged for participation are kept at one-third of true Programme cost. In addition, partial scholarships based on need are awarded to small museums to facilitate their participation. The remaining funds to support the Programme have been provided by public and private sources. Major contributors have included the Compton Foundation, the William H. Donner Foundation, The Andrew W. Mellon Foundation, the Mabel Pew Myrin Trust, the Alfred P. Sloan Foundation, the National Endowment for the Arts and the New York State Council on the Arts. Additional funding has been received from fourteen corporations and two private foundations.

The Practicum projects executed by participants provide insight into the management problems faced by American museums and reveal how museum administrators have been able to resolve, or at least manage, these problems.

Several themes connect many of the projects that have been completed over the years. Upon examination, these themes seem to exemplify principles of effective management — concepts taught in the Programme — and it is no coincidence that they surface repeatedly.

One is the need to establish or clarify an institution's overall direction and to actively plan its future. The need to know where an institution is heading is profound. It is this understanding that keeps an institution on course, that enables museum staff and Board members to "pull in the same direction", and that provides the rationale for acceptance or rejection of programme and exhibit proposals.

It is not surprising, then, that the most common Practicum project undertaken is the creation or updating of a strategic plan. This plan, which essentially identifies where an institution wishes to be in three to five years, and provides a "road map" for getting there by providing clear goals and measurable objectives along the way, furnishes the guidance and direction that is so desperately sought. For the same reason, another very common Practicum project is the establishment or revision of an institution's mission statement, an effort that is often undertaken as a first step in the strategic planning process.

A second theme is the importance of examining and evaluating established structures, policies and procedures. For their Practicum projects, many participants have reviewed institutional structures and procedures, and, finding that what was in place was unsatisfactory, have developed new ones. The most common reason for such changes was that the existing structures or procedures were not supportive of, or consistent with, newly developed or clarified institutional goals or objectives. Although some react negatively to changing "the way things have always been done", effective managers realize that such revision is often necessary. Implicit here is the idea that an institution must not be afraid of change nor be the victim of change, but rather must plan for and manage change. Along these lines, we encounter Practicum projects dealing with staff reorganizations, revisions of personnel policies and practices, and the establishment of more formalized procedures in young and rapidly growing organizations.

A third theme is the desire to base decisions on the most accurate and relevant information available. The goal is to avoid decisions that are arbitrary or autocratic, as well as those based solely on tradition. To this end, in executing their Practicum projects, many museum managers have employed marketing research techniques such as focus groups, telephone and mail surveys, in-person interviews and programme evaluations to

gather information about market needs and interests, prior to decision making. Specifically, the information gathered often concerns the institution's image, its audience or potential audience, or the appeal of projects designed to earn income. By securing this information, museum managers are able to anticipate the public's response to various projects, and can choose the one with the greatest likelihood of success.

A fourth theme among Practicum projects is the desire to take advantage of opportunities and to anticipate and prepare for obstacles and challenges. In its broadest interpretation, this follows logically from the elements of the strategic planning process that emphasize analysis of the external environment and assessment of internal strengths and weaknesses. All of the strategic plans developed as Practicum projects reflect this theme.

On a more programmatic level, this attitude encourages entrepreneurship and opportunism (in the positive sense), and requires that managers examine the expected positive and negative consequences of various actions, choose a course of action based on careful analysis, and then take the steps needed to maximize positive outcomes and minimize negative ones. In the Practicum projects this idea is reflected, for example, in planning committees that involve key community members so that their support is assured, and in studies that seek to identify an institution's competitive or differential advantage in relation to other cultural institutions, both for planning and promotional purposes.

The final theme found in the projects is the desire to use resources wisely. In terms of

A group of visitors examine the Missal of St. Francis *in a special exhibition at the Walters Art Gallery.*

be allocated so as to do the most good, thereby enabling the institutions to do a few things very well rather than many things poorly — the "Jack of All Trades, Master of None" syndrome. In this vein, too, we see analyses of programmes designed to raise or earn funds as well as those intended to reduce costs.

In all, the projects are extremely ambitious endeavours that have had profound effects on museum management policies and practices. Summaries of fourteen Practicum projects follow.

The Assistant Director of the Newark Museum felt that several changes in the structure of the organization were needed. The table of organization, shaped over the years to accommodate the talents, expertise and longevity of the staff, was felt to be outmoded. Lines of responsibility were unclear following the retirement of senior administrators, and tasks were often accomplished only because of the extraordinary sense of responsibility of most members of the Museum staff. The need for change was magnified by the impending physical expansion of the Museum, which had brought about an examination of the philosophy and mission of the institution. For his Practicum project, the Assistant Director created a new table of organization which clearly separated and defined the function of each department and each position within it, as well as defining how each department related to others in the Museum. He worked with members of every division and department to create mission statements for each one. He further recommended new structures and formats for staff meetings to ensure communication relating to the Museum's goals, strategies and operations. Staff members came to appreciate having predictable, periodic opportunities to

managing human resources, many projects document efforts to communicate institutional goals and objectives at all levels of the organization, to clarify the roles and responsibilities of staff and Board members, and to establish mechanisms to monitor performance. All are intended to give each individual an understanding of how he or she fits into the organization, to ensure commonality of vision and to increase productivity. In terms of managing financial resources, many projects focused on making choices among alternative options or limiting an institution's range of activities. This was done so that scarce financial resources could examine their goals and gauge their success. All in all, since implementing these changes, communication is far more efficient and effective, and the 'climate' of the organization is vastly improved.

The Executive Director of The Horticultural Society of New York focused on formulating a long-range plan for the Society, the first the organization had ever had. He perceived that the Society had reached a plateau and felt that a decision was needed regarding its future: should it continue as it was or should it move in a new direction? The external environment was analyzed to determine what impact the economy, politics, society and technology were having or might have on The Horticultural Society, and to assess the challenges and opportunities these forces brought with them. The Director also analyzed the organization's internal strengths and weaknesses, and examined these elements in relation to the Society's direct competitors. By conducting a marketing survey of Society members, the organization discovered which of their programmes were most appealing. All of this information was incorporated into the new plan, which, although still supportive of the institution's basic mission, charted some new directions for the Society. In keeping with their new and clearly-stated goals and objectives, certain programmes were de-emphasized or eliminated, while a major activity, the International Flower Show, was revived. The Society's Board and staff were both integrally involved in developing the plan, the latter being re-organized to facilitate the plan's implementation.

The Director of the University of Kentucky Art Museum in Lexington focused on formulating an audience development strategy for his four year old institution. His goal was to reach new market segments and increase regular visits, as well as to build the Museum's financial base. For his Practicum project he conducted a series of focus groups with representatives of various segments of the community to learn their perceptions of the Museum and to have them evaluate current and potential programmes and services. This was followed by a questionnaire which was mailed to Museum members and distributed in person to Museum visitors.

The focus groups and questionnaires revealed that, in general, the public was quite satisfied with the Museum's programmes and exhibitions. There was, however, a serious image problem, resulting mainly from the Museum's association with the University, which for years had maintained a decided aloofness from its community. In the months following the study, the Museum took several steps to counteract this problem, including hiring a public relations professional, meeting with key corporate leaders on an on-going basis, altering the composition of the Board of Trustees to achieve greater community representation, and working with the Mayor of Lexington on a series of art projects so that the community-at-large could view the institution as a community museum in an academic setting rather than as a university museum. The change in the public's perception of the Museum was reflected in a substantial increase in visits and contributions.

The Vice-Director for Education at The Brooklyn Museum had become increasingly concerned about the drop in the Museum's art school enrolment, which had resulted in reduced income for the division. This was due, in part, to the proliferation of competitors

First person interpretation in the "Mysteries in History" gallery of the Children's Museum of Indianapolis.

school exceeded its earned income projection by 25%.

The Director of the St. Louis County Historical Society in Duluth, Minnesota prepared a detailed analysis of shared staffing opportunities between his institution and the Lake Superior Transportation Museum, both of which are housed within the St. Louis County Heritage and Arts Center complex. The project resulted in a plan to centralize the administration and merge the operations of the two institutions. This arrangement not only saved the institutions approximately $35,000 each year (18% of their combined budgets), but also entitled them to receive a large subsidy from the State of Minnesota, enabling them to hire needed personnel — a full-time curator, an exhibits designer and an additional secretary.

The relatively new Director of The Walters Art Gallery in Baltimore, Maryland quickly discovered that in all the years of the museum's existence, there had never been a formal organizational chart. This had resulted in confusion among the staff as to lines of authority and fear regarding the exercise of that authority. More importantly, the Director realized that if the museum was to implement its newly-formulated strategy of changing from a "high-brow" institution to one that was responsive to a broader public, it needed to dramatically change its organizational structure. For his Practicum project, the Director identified weaknesses in the current structure and proposed a revised system that was more supportive of, and consistent with, the institution's new goals. This included creating new departments and reorganizing many of the existing ones. The plan was welcomed by Board and staff alike and the institution is now in a much better position to realize its objectives.

— other cultural institutions and schools offering similar programmes for the public in the same geographical area. For his Practicum project, the division head analyzed the art school's portfolio of offerings to see which were most lucrative. He then compared the Museum's programmes to those of its competitors by carrying out a perceived value analysis. From these analyses, he realized that the Museum school had a distinct advantage on which it was not capitalizing: the collections, as well as high quality and extremely popular temporary exhibitions. A new strategy was developed — to plan courses around the Museum's exhibition programme, and to incorporate the collections and exhibits into the various offerings. Implementing this plan, which required major changes in how the art school marketed its programmes, almost immediately resulted in higher school enrolments, increased revenue and a general revitalization of the school. For the year in which these changes were introduced, the

The Coordinator of Development at Sleepy Hollow Restorations in Tarrytown, New York conducted a market research survey on a proposed series of workshops to take place during the museum's "slow months". The study covered course content, structure and pricing, and elicited enough information to initiate a very successful programme, which has been offered in subsequent years in an expanded form. Unlike many museum education programmes, the series was designed for adults, reflecting current demographic trends. The workshops were not only effective programmatically, but served to bring additional visitors to the museum during times of traditionally low visitation. More importantly, workshop participants were solicited for museum membership, thus increasing income on two fronts. This effort at generating earned income constituted a new era of involvement for Sleepy Hollow, which had previously been almost exclusively dependent on its endowment.

The Vice-Director for Education at The Metropolitan Museum of Art in New York City identified a mission for education within the Museum and devised a plan by which the five departments which comprise the Division of Education Services were reorganized for increased efficiency and effectiveness. This has resulted in improved management of the Division and in more innovative and responsive programming for the diverse publics it serves.

The Director of Collections at The Children's Museum of Indianapolis focused on developing a long range plan for his department of the Museum. His participation in the programme also enabled him to help other department heads with their plans. All of

these were then synthesized to create an institutional five year plan, the first the Museum ever had. The planning process brought about an evaluation and subsequent redefinition of the Museum's mission, which enabled the staff to measure the institution's past performance as well as to set clear and consistent goals for the future. The plan was enthusiastically received by the Museum's Board of Directors and is currently being implemented.

The Museum of Holography, located in New York City, was founded with a two-person staff and a budget of $86,000 and grew to have a nine-person staff and a budget of $600,000 in four years. This sudden growth necessitated many changes in policy and practice. Human resources management was one area which had been relatively neglected and was the focus of the Practicum project executed by the Museum's Director. A review of present practices and an analysis of future goals revealed the need to reorganize the departments within the Museum, revise job descriptions and functions, and institute quarterly reviews where objectives would be established. Implementing these recommendations resulted in a stronger and more stable institution.

The Curator of American Paintings and Sculpture at The Brooklyn Museum analyzed the feasibility and attractiveness of establishing a Friends of American Art group for the Museum. The impetus for the project came from the fact that a Friends group could help to raise the profile of the institution in general, and of these collections in particular. The funds raised would be used for acquisitions, research or conservation work within that department. For her project, the Curator surveyed museums throughout the country which have such support groups, to better understand their structure, features and the benefits and liabilities associated with them. From the research it was learned that these groups had done much to raise visibility and generate funds, but that the necessary administrative work could be a burden on the curatorial staff. Armed with this information, in her proposal the Curator recommended a structure whereby the curatorial department would be responsible for the content of Friends events, but the membership department would handle administrative matters. Her proposal was accepted, and several months later, the newly formed group launched its first event. The Director of the Museum, eager for the visibility and revenue, viewed the effort as a pilot project which, if successful, would be emulated by other departments within the Museum.

The Regional Historic Preservation Supervisor of the Palisades Interstate Park Commission of New York State sought to introduce more rational and effective budget preparation techniques to the various historic sites within the region. Four alternative approaches were analyzed. The one selected combined increasing communication between the Regional Historic Preservation Supervisor and the site managers regarding New York State's budget process, redefining the respective roles of the Supervisor and the site managers vis-a-vis budget preparation, and instituting procedures for monitoring expenses. The plan resulted in increased efficiency and in the achievement of newly-prioritized goals.

The Director of a medium-sized art museum in California utilized the human resources management curriculum to focus on a situation involving a key staff member who formerly had been a member of the Museum's Board of Trustees. By various means, the staff member was attempting to maintain her influence on the Board, although she had relinquished her status as a Board member when she assumed the staff position. Rectifying this problem required the Museum Director to more clearly define and communicate the distinct roles and responsibilities of staff members and Board members as well as to establish performance evaluation policies within the institution.

In an effort to increase visitation at the Roberson Center for Arts and Sciences in Binghamton, New York, the Manager of Public Relations embarked on a market research project involving representatives of the local tourism industry (motel owners, car rental agencies, merchant associations, etc.) and community development leaders. The study sought to determine the Center's role in attracting tourists and residents to the Binghamton area and to evaluate potential methods of communication between the Center and the local tourism industry. The research revealed that the target population was quite willing to support and promote the Center's activities and underscored the need for increased communication between the two groups. The involvement of the tourism industry and of community development leaders increased the Center's visitation and laid the foundation for fundraising appeals to local businesses based on Roberson's key role in the community.

This final section will address programme philosophy, operating assumptions, and the rationale for certain decisions and practices. The format will be to provide answers to frequently asked questions. By way of back-ground, in making many of the initial decisions regarding curriculum, faculty and programme structure, the staff of Museums Collaborative was guided by responses to a needs analysis survey it administered to several hundred former participants in workshops sponsored by the Collaborative, as well as by an Advisory Council comprised of museum professionals and representatives of the business and academic communities, assembled expressly for this purpose.

How was the target audience determined?

The target audience evolved from carefully considering the goals and objectives of the Programme and how they might best be achieved. Since the central goal was to improve the management of cultural institutions, the most efficient and effective way of accomplishing this seemed to be to provide management training for the people currently in key decision-making positions within these institutions — Directors, Deputy Directors and department heads. While the training might have been targeted at more junior personnel, these individuals would not be in positions to put the training to use until much later in their careers. The target audience was comprised of those who could have an immediate and enduring impact on management practices within their institutions. Apart from this, it was felt that to provide training in management techniques to individuals who, due to their positions had not yet experienced any significant management problems or puzzled over thorny management decisions, would not be fruitful. Management concepts are best taught to those who can connect the ideas to their own real world experiences.

Why were faculty members all from leading business schools? Why was there no museum representation?

Once the target audience was determined, this decision was relatively easy, although not without ramifications. It was felt that while some museum directors were, in fact, excellent managers, most had learned what they do through trial and error, rather than through formal training. Consequently, they are frequently unable to conceptualize or generalize about management theory and practice. Moreover, good managers are not necessarily good teachers; it was essential that the faculty be knowledgeable about management concepts, and equally important that they be able to communicate them. Faculty members drawn from graduate schools of business brought just this combination of assets, and, in addition, satisfied participants' need for credibility and prestige.

That the busines school professors selected did not (when the programme started) have a thorough knowledge of museums was felt to be a drawback that could be fairly easily remedied by working closely with the Museums Collaborative staff and utilizing their experience with other not-for-profit institutions.

From an educational and programmatic point of view, the decision to utilize business school professors proved to be an excellent one. From a political and marketing perspective, it was not. When the staff began marketing the Programme, it became evident that many "senior statesmen" of the profession felt they should have been called upon to serve as faculty, and were not willing to be overly supportive of the Programme. Others wondered if a business school faculty could understand their needs and if the curriculum would be relevant.

Respondents to the needs assessment survey were emphatic about the fact that they could not be absent from their institutions for more than a week at a time. They also clearly expressed a desire to practically apply the concepts and skills presented. These two elements were incorporated into the Programme's design. Because of the time restriction, it was decided that it would be best for participants to be in residence at a retreat-type conference centre during the intial component (the Institute). In this way, distractions were minimized and evening sessions could be scheduled, allowing more material to be covered. Also, this permitted participants to get to know one another and the faculty more quickly, and facilitated participants learning from each other through informal sharing of management experiences.

The interior ramp system of The Children's Museum of Indianapolis.

In point of fact, in the initial presentation of the *Principles of Management for Cultural Institutions* course, a prominent museum director was included on the faculty as a presenter and to "translate" business concepts into museum language, if needed. From the evaluations, it was quite apparent that participants felt the translation function to be unnecessary and that they already had sufficient access to museum professionals both within the course (fellow participants) and without. As senior museum professionals themselves, they indicated they did not feel a need to hear from "one of their own"; rather, what they wanted were perspectives from outside the museum field. As the Programme continued and its reputation became established, concerns about the faculty on the part of prospective applicants disappeared due to awareness of the positive experiences of past participants.

The Practicum project seemed an ideal way to satisfy participants' desire for immediate application of the curriculum. The execution of the project, combined with two opportunities to analyze fellow participants' projects (at the Interim Meeting and the concluding Seminar), enabled participants to sharpen their problem-solving skills, and significantly increased the likelihood that these techniques and skills would continue to be used.

That the friendships which developed among participants, faculty and Museum Collaborative staff often continued for months and years after courses had concluded reflects the candour and closeness this structure fostered. Participants saw these relationships as safe and supportive, and knew that if they called on a fellow participant, for example, to discuss alternative solutions to a particular

The Horticultural Society of New York — the New York Flower Show: the Garden of the Pools.

problem, they would receive an honest, sincere and well-reasoned response, just as they had when the course was in progress.

How were the content areas included in the curriculum selected?

Curriculum development was mainly the responsibility of the faculty, who had been hired for their management expertise and experience in training executives. Guided by the recommendations of the Advisory Council and the results of the needs assessment survey, the faculty worked closely with Museums Collaborative staff members to ensure that the curriculum would be relevant to museum administrators.

Apart from the overriding concern for relevance and responsiveness to needs, the factor that most governed the selection process was time. Every effort was made to include essentials and avoid inclusion of any topics which were being adequately addressed in other training programmes. In the *Principles of Management for Cultural Institutions* course, for example, topics such as legal concerns and the use of computers in management were eliminated. The curriculum finally arrived at emphasized strategic planning, and covered topics such as financial management, marketing, and human resources management as tools to enable an institution to achieve its plan.

Museum professionals often ask why we did not include fundraising as part of the programme. The reason for this is two-fold. First, there were and are many excellent training programmes available on this subject. Second, and of greater importance, there was a bias among the Museums Collaborative staff and the faculty that dictated that we encourage entrepreneurship and the independence that comes with self-sufficiency; our emphasis was therefore on developing earned income rather than on grantsmanship. This approach proved to be effective as well as timely when government and corporate support of cultural institutions was substantially reduced.

The *Marketing for Audience and Income Development* and *Managing Human Resources for Organizational Effectiveness* curricula were developed along similar lines. For all three courses, participant evaluations, administered twice during each course, provided the guidelines for revision.

What issues affected the marketing of the Programme?
The Programme has been formally marketed via direct mail, press releases in professional newsletters and journals, distribution of brochures at professional meetings and telephone. However, the most effective marketing tool probably has been the word of mouth endorsement of former participants to their colleagues. Receptivity to the Programme grew due to its reputation for quality, relevance and impact among museum professionals.

Changes in the funding environment also affected museum professionals' attitudes towards the Programme. As funding became increasingly difficult to obtain, there seemed

to be a greater recognition of how essential sound management is to an institution's survival and growth. Along with this realization came greater interest in management training as a means of strengthening the managerial performance of key personnel.

The fact that other programmes were subsequently developed, that were in competition with the Cultural Institutions Management Programme, also affected its marketing. Specifically, every effort was made to distinguish the Programme from its competitors and, when asked, to help a prospective applicant to select the programme that would best meet his or her needs. The chief differentiating factors were the background and calibre of the faculty, the structure of the Programme – requiring the execution of a Practicum project, and the level of participants the Programme attracted – far more senior than any other programme.

Obtaining funding for the Programme, to subsidize the registration fees paid by the participants, required a different marketing approach. For government agencies and private foundations, the proven benefits to the target audience seemed sufficient to gain their support. For corporations, however, particularly those which directly supported cultural institutions, it was often necessary to demonstrate that providing funding for the Cultural Institutions Management Programme could protect their investment in those institutions.

The Cultural Institutions Management Programme is an innovative approach to museum management training that has resulted in significantly improved management in participating institutions. The keys to its effectiveness and success lie in carefully defined eligibility criteria, especially with regard to the nature and scope of applicants' management responsibilities, faculty members who combine knowledge of not-for-profit management with long experience in communicating these concepts to senior executives, a structure that requires participants to apply aspects of the curriculum to actual management problems within their institutions, and the use of on-going evaluation to ensure that the Programme remains responsive to the needs of the museum field.

The Horticultural Society of New York — the New York Flower Show: entrance pavilion, "Paradise in the Sun".

The same influences which gave rise to a strong independent sector also led to a friendly attitude on the part of our government towards that sector. The American income tax structure, to this day, encourages giving. With the Reagan administration's energetic drive to reduce the role of government, private giving by individuals, foundations and corporations is in the limelight more than ever before. Our phrase, "your contribution is deductible for tax purposes" is music to the ears of every American arts administrator.

But, as the American newpaper editor Walter Lippman said, "Opinions can prevail only if the facts to which they refer are known". So I will try to illustrate much of what I say with a number of statistics which will help to suggest trends and areas of emphasis in American philanthropy as it relates to support of the arts.

In 1984, the total amount spent by the federal government in the United States on arts programmes was about $500 million. This is an impressive figure, but less impressive than the $600 million given to the arts by American businesses. About 19% of those funds donated by businesses went to museums. But while corporate giving topped government support by $100 million, individual donations to the arts are almost incalculable. The American Association of Fund-Raising Counsel puts philanthropic donations to the arts by individuals and foundations at $5.4 *billion* in 1984, exactly twice as much as just five years earlier. This all comes down to about twelve dollars given each year by every American.

Some of this can be attributed, of course, to an American bias toward culture and cultural events. It is interesting to note that 58% of Americans attended an art musem last year, and 27% of all adults in the country made an average contribution to the arts of $50. Many of you have seen the result of this emphasis on the arts in the United States in the exhibits and events of the American Festival which has been taking place in Great Britain this summer.

Most American museums receive no more money from the public purse than comparable museums in Great Britain, except for the Smithsonian Institution and the National Gallery in Washington, which receive more than $200 million each year. American museums have been known, in fact, to look enviously across the Atlantic at the British system of government subsidy, which is

Philanthropic donations to the arts in the United States in 1984 demonstrate overwhelming support from individuals.

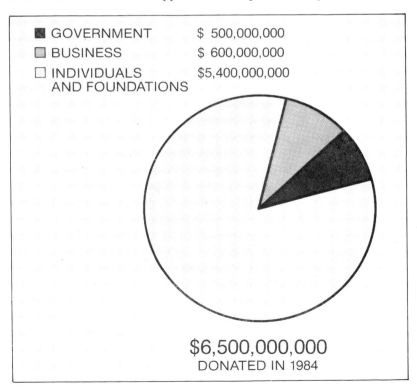

■ GOVERNMENT	$ 500,000,000
▨ BUSINESS	$ 600,000,000
☐ INDIVIDUALS AND FOUNDATIONS	$5,400,000,000

$6,500,000,000
DONATED IN 1984

considered by many to promote stability and the freedom to experiment — even to fail occasionally.

In 1985, the National Endowment for the Arts and the Arts Council of Great Britain had roughly comparable budgets. The difference between government subsidy of museums in Great Britain and the United States lies not in the amount, but in the way that money is ultimately spent. American museums tend to use the support they receive to raise more money through techniques such as challenge grant programmes, which increasingly involve sophisticated marketing and public relations. The result is that government grants generate more income in America than they do here. To compare two institutions similar in size, for instance: $20 million in grants to the Metropolitan Museum of Art in New York City in 1983 generated $28 million in additional income. A similar subsidy to the British Museum and the National Gallery that year generated £1.3 million, only one sixteenth as much!

The various ways that 'other income' is generated by American museums will form the substance of my comments to you. Some of the methods I describe will be merely interesting, rather than directly relevant to your situation. Your tax system, the requirements of covenanting and the phenomenon of 'clawing back' create a very different climate for you — to say nothing of the political considerations involved in corporate and individual contributions. On the other hand, I know that you and your trustees and legislators are studying the problem, so change may be in the wind.

I believe strongly that the American public is no better disposed toward philanthropy than is your constituency. Those colonists I mentioned earlier had, after all, strong roots in the Anglo-Saxon tradition. Where deductability has been permitted in Britain in the area of corporate sponsorship of the arts, for instance, it has been just as much an incentive to giving as it has in America. Business sponsorship for the arts in Britain has, I understand, jumped from £250,000 in 1972 to £14 million in 1984 — roughly the same percentage increase that we have experienced in that sector in America.

Simon Jenkins, in his November 1984 article in *The Economist*, entitled "Paying for the Arts" said, "The success of corporate sponsorship and membership fund-raising by unsubsidized institutions in Great Britain suggests that there is … a large sleeping constituency of private individual support for the arts waiting to be roused". Mr. Jenkins was not anticipating that one of the constituents would hail from the United States. The gift of $62.5 million by J. Paul Getty II to the National Gallery has been, as you might imagine, a great boost to that museum's support drive.

My plan, then, is to tell you about how we raise funds in America with the hope that some of our ideas might help you to awaken any sleeping constituency you might have here in Scotland and throughout Britain. With cuts in arts support here, in my country, and in Canada and Australia, we find ourselves in the midst of an era of shifting priorities and new approaches to funding.

America's 5,500 museums had budgets totalling about $1.5 billion in 1984. The most recent comprehensive survey published by the National Endowment for the Arts tells us quite a bit about how museums get and spend their money. Of the income received by

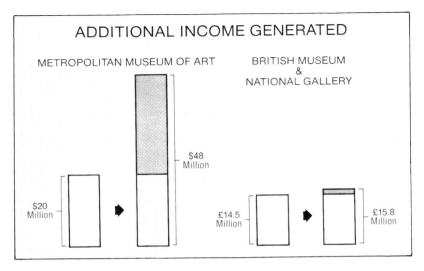

ADDITIONAL INCOME GENERATED

METROPOLITAN MUSEUM OF ART

BRITISH MUSEUM
&
NATIONAL GALLERY

$48
Million

$20
Million

£14.5
Million

£15.8
Million

At the Metropolitan Museum of Art, sophisticated marketing techniques such as the challenge grant programme more than double support from a $20 million government grant.

museums, approximately 63% was provided by the private sector, and 37% by the public sector. Private sector support came from contributions from individuals, foundations, corporations, membership funds and allocations from colleges and universities. Almost half of all contributions came from individuals.

Additional support for American museums was generated by such things as admission fees, sales from museum shops, licensing programmes, and revenues from special facilities such as parking lots and restaurants. All in all, these operating revenues contributed 29% of the total income to museums.

Those same museums spent their money primarily in five different areas: 28% went on administrative expenses, 27% on operations and support, 20% on curatorial, display and exhibit activities, 15% on education, and 10% on research. Income from the public sector included funds from municipal and

county government, which provided 18% of the total, state government (7%), and federal government (12%).

These figures give you an interesting view of the economics of museums in America. They don't, however, reflect the recent changes that have been taking place in many of America's great old arts institutions. The Metropolitan Museum, for instance, relied on endowment income for 70% of its revenue as recently as 25 years ago. Today, endowment income has shrunk to just 15% of its total income.

By contrast contributions (including admissions, membership fees, and private gifts and grants) were over half of that museum's budget in 1984. Auxiliary activities, such as retail and catering, yielded $3 million. At the Museum of Modern Art in New York, $5.2 million of a $7.7 million operating income came from admissions and members, while only $1 million came from government grants.

You can imagine, in light of these statistics, how much emphasis is placed on fund-raising activities in American museums. Fund-raising never stops, and to many administrators, it seems like their primary responsibility. Museum membership is, of course, one of the primary sources of yearly repeated support.

All American museums rely on membership drives — many of which are quite ingenious in character. The Met doubled its membership in the last five years by using many of the most popular membership drive techniques. Members almost always receive something fairly tangible in return for joining. They are offered a kind of hierarchy of privileges and honours related to the scale of their giving — including reduced admission rates, monthly newsletters, invitations to special events and openings, and even small gifts such as scarves, pins, or tote bags. Members are made to feel a real part of the institution they have joined.

Annual giving represents the ongoing commitment of the museum's constituency. Members form the lion's share of those who contribute to the annual giving programme, but annual giving programmes appeal to a much larger constituency. Annual giving is conducted by about six different methods, but most museums combine several of these ways, and some use all of them. The first is to encourage giving on an annual basis through face-to-face solicitation — which is, after all, the basic model of modern philanthropy. The museum volunteer directly confronts the prospect and asks for support. The success of this request often depends on the volunteer's enthusiasm and dedication. It is therefore considered extremely worthwhile to develop a strong relationship with a loyal group of volunteers upon which a museum's fund-raising success may ultimately rest.

Another popular annual giving appeal often takes the form of a simple letter from the organization's executive director, president, board chairman, or another volunteer. The letter is often accompanied by a progress report or a brochure which describes the museum's recent efforts. Direct mail packages are also central to annual giving programmes. These range from simple letters to printed packages complete with brochures, response cards, return envelopes, and sometimes even bumper stickers or buttons. Phonathons, or events in which volunteers call potential donors on the telephone and ask directly for a gift to reach an established goal, are an effective method of increasing annual support, as are gift clubs which establish categories of

giving levels and encourage donors to become part of a special group which supports the museum.

Museum staff usually take the necessary time and effort to build a strong annual giving programme. Through these programmes, museums build a solid volunteer body which is informed about its collections and programmes, and can communicate with the other members of the museum's constituency. Major donor prospects are often uncovered through annual giving programmes, and a strong annual membership is an encouragement and a challenge to foundations and corporations to offer matching funds.

Annual giving programmes in America are becoming as creative and innovative as the organizations themselves. Some develop specialized programmes to reach specific audiences such as corporate campaigns or challenge programmes in which an individual or a corporation challenges the rest of the museum's constituency by matching new annual gifts. The challenge might be on a dollar-for-dollar basis or a promise to donate a certain amount if a particular goal is reached.

Most museum fund raisers would agree that deferred gifts are an excellent, though often unexplored, means of meeting the financial challenges that non-profit organizations face. Deferred giving is something akin to your process of covenanting except that the donor receives tremendous benefit from choosing this route of giving. The donor receives a tax benefit and, in some cases, income for life (if an annuity or charitable remainder trust is established, for example). The museum is also assured of future income, and can plan its programmes and budgets accordingly.

Of course, one of the most popular and fully developed sources of yearly, repeated support for museums in America is foundation funding. Recently, the Internal Revenue Service estimated that there are approximately 28,000 foundations in the United States authorized to operate as private, grant-making agencies. Since these foundations exist solely in order to give money away, there is a great deal of information available on them, and the avenues to funding requests are well-paved — and, unfortunately sometimes, well-travelled.

Foundations gave more than $88 million to American museums in 1982-83. $33 million of that total went to capital support; close to $21 million was for continuing support; almost $19 million was for general or operating support; and about the same went to programme development. The state which received the most money from foundations was New York, with grants totalling more than $20 million; but Texas was right behind New York with more than $16 million. Even though the Texas oil boom seems to have ended, the Texas economy is still fertile ground for arts institutions. As Brian O'Reilly said in a recent article in *Fortune* magazine, "Texas may be running out of oil, but Texans sure aren't running out of energy."

Foundations are usually approached for funds through a written proposal which gives background on the museum, describes its current programming, and proposes a series of goals needing support. A budget is always included with a proposal, and usually a request for a specific amount of support as well. Corporations are approached in much the same way. Each year corporations are becoming a more important source of funding for non-profit organizations in America. In 1979, for the first time, corporate contributions exceeded those of foundations. Corporations allocate funds through corporate foundations, contributions committees, and matching gift programmes in which companies match gifts made to museums by their employees. Corporate and foundation donors usually appreciate an ongoing relationship with an institution they fund, and often request follow-up communications and progress reports.

Capital fund-raising campaigns are a common way for American museums to raise large sums of money for the construction of new facilities and for increasing their endowment. Campaigns are being conducted with a greater level of sophistication and planning. There is always a plan for the campaign, which includes charts, timetables and budgets. A 'Case for Support' is developed early on, and usually takes the form of an eloquent and fully explanatory statement in writing of the institution's objectives, history, needs and plans for the future. An intense programme of cultivation of individual prospects and activities related to the campaign go hand-in-hand. As always, however, the success of face-to-face solicitation is the backbone of any museum campaign. Researching the prospects who will be approached by volunteers — and cultivating them — is the trickiest and most important campaign activity that goes on.

As I mentioned earlier, American museums have been branching out into other areas of fund-raising beyond these rather traditional methods. Museum shops have become common resources for Americans shopping for Christmas gifts and mementos of their visit to a particular city. Shops sell reproductions, books, postcards and even jewellery and toys for children. Museums also earn income through admissions, of course, and through organizing special trips or tours for their members. Publishing programmes are often a profit-making arm of a museum, with the materials produced being compatible with the museum's image and specific area of interest.

Licensing programmes are also becoming increasingly popular with museum administrators. These programmes link nationally respected museums with equally regarded manufacturers and retailers who, under strict control, are empowered to manufacture and market reproductions and other products based on museum collection designs. In return for these rights, the licensee pays royalties to the museum for the length of a contract. Contracts are negotiated for the museum by a licensing agent and are renewed and exended when the appropriate time comes — if the museum is happy with the arrangement, of course. This new direction in museum merchandising is credited with bringing designs of artistic merit to the American marketplace, and a mass audience into America's museums. Income from licensing and marketing can be very substantial indeed.

In order to be successful in many of the areas of fund-raising I have described, there is one element which museum administrators are learning is all important. As commercial advertising becomes more and more dominant in our country, museum staff members are realizing that in order to attract a wide general public, they must use strong, simple, or even colourful messages. They are realizing, in other words, that they must become experts at public relations. The success of many campaigns for museums has been invaluably assisted by attractive and well-written campaign materials, such as Case Statements and articles in newspapers which co-incide with the launching of a campaign. Audio-visual presentations which bring the museum to life through a well-produced show made up of slides or video and music and narration are used in most campaigns to introduce meetings, special events, or even private solicitations.

Another aspect of museum campaigns which is growing in importance and sophistication is the actual mechanics of raising the campaign funds. These include setting up a well-organized development office in the museum with a staff which researches and identifies prospects. This is where the museum's Board of Trustees and volunteers come into play. When the right prospects have been properly identified, those close to the museum approach prospects they know or friends of those prospects in order to secure a meeting.

Trustees and volunteers meet frequently during a campaign to exchange information about prospects and to review the progress they are making in reaching and meeting each of those who has been identified. It is impossible to over-estimate the importance of the museum volunteer in this process. Since these people are already committed to the museum and have the respect of their peers, they are best qualified to solicit support from others. They are always treated well by the museum, trained carefully, and armed with strong written materials which help them to complete their task. In campaigns, volunteers are organized into committees which meet to review progress and set goals to be reached.

It is not surprising that, when considering a campaign or improved approach to yearly

*Attractive and colourful
fund-raising materials
provide invaluable
assistance to the overall
success of a campaign.*

fund-raising, museum administrators often turn to fund-raising consultants to plan, organize, motivate, offer support and back-up, and generally take responsibility for the guidance of the fund-raising programmes. Consultants rarely perform actual solicitations, mainly because they will not be nearly so effective as volunteers who are intimate with the museum. But they do become involved in virtually every other aspect of a campaign, conduct feasibility or planning studies, produce a wide variety of materials for use in campaigns, and offer advice and encouragement to the museum and its staff.

Fund-raising is an art which is not always practiced well or successfully, of course. I do believe that it is closer to an art than a science, and it is — and will remain — a very personal business. When all is said and done, it is likely that museums will choose consultants whom the trustees and administrators like and respect for past efforts and associations. Many consultants are an integral part of the cultural scene in America, serving first one institution, then another as special needs arise. The museums and the consultants have one common goal: to make each museum in America the best museum that it can be.

American museums are expanding every day, hopefully no further than they can or should. I hope that my description of the various ways we raise funds in America will be of some help to you as you labour to bring your own museums here in Scotland and throughout Britain to the height of their full growth and glory.

In the Metropolitan Museum
of Art, New York.

The Smithsonian Kellogg Project

Jane R. Glaser

During the past two years, a number of major reports have come out on the state and quality of American education, including a report from the Carnegie Foundation and the report of the National Commission on Excellence in Education, titled "A Nation at Risk". Most of these reports, while reviewing America's educational resources, did not mention museums as being among these resources. "A Nation at Risk", which noted museums in passing, briefly alluded to their educational potential.

About five years ago the W.K. Kellogg Foundation, the fourth largest foundation in the United States, discovered the educational power of museums when one of its programme directors, paid a visit to The Exploratorium in San Francisco, the participatory science museum learning centre developed by Dr. Frank Oppenheimer. Excited by this alternative to traditional learning, the director pressed the Kellogg Foundation to award a grant to The Exploratorium to conduct residencies whereby other museum professionals could spend a period of time at The Exploratorium, studying its methods of creating a learning environment through participatory exhibits; these professionals would presumably develop their own exhibits upon returning to their home institutions. This Kellogg grant programme has continued over the past four years.

In 1982, the W.K. Kellogg Foundation awarded two additional grants to further expand the potential of education in museums. One was to the Field Museum of Natural History in Chicago, which has conducted a series of workshops for museum professionals on the team approach to exhibition planning. The other grant was to the Smithsonian Institution's Office of Museum Programs, to "expand the educational role of museums in their communities".

How was this to be done — "to expand the educational role of museums in their communities"?

The issues are not new, what is new is the way in which the issues must be addressed. This is best described by explaining some of the working philosophies of the Smithsonian Kellogg project.

The first philosophical stance is that all activities of a museum are intimately related to the educational function of a museum, that is, the creation of an environment for learning in the museum — the presentation to the public of the tools and resources by which that learning can take place. We view research and exhibition and aesthetic contemplation as elements of that educational purpose. If those who examine American education, who write about education, who pass laws and make money available for education, and who participate in education don't recognize museums as educational institutions, as part of the educational process in the United States then we as museum professionals have a lot of educating to do — educating of the pundits, of the press, of the politicos, and, of course, of the public itself.

The understanding and the practice of public education in a museum must not be solely the responsibility of an education department, but must involve all departments and personnel of the museum, *including the director*.

A second philosophical stance, therefore, is that the museum director must be involved in, and oversee, the museum's educational activities if education is to take its rightful place in the museum and receive its proper share of support. Only a director can ensure balanced co-ordination in the following key areas: contributions of expertise and research findings from the curatorial staff, the participation of the education staff in the early stages of planning of both exhibitions and publications, and increased access by the public, both physically and intellectually, to the collections and staff expertise of the museum.

This leads to the third philosophical stance, namely, that museums must develop educational policy statements, much as they have learned to develop overall mission statements and collections policies. In these they must state in down-to-earth and practical terms their relationship to the educational life of their communities.

The fourth philosophical stance is that museums must actively and continually work to educate the public about museums and how to use them. Around the age of six we are taught to read books, and thereupon begin to learn to use both the classroom and the public library as learning environments, but nowhere along the line are we taught how to use the museum, the primary focus of which is objects, as a learning environment. The public must be taught how it can use the museum's resources for learning and self-study.

The fifth and final philosophical stance is that in doing this, museums must co-operate and collaborate more regularly with other educational institutions in their communities, namely, the schools, the colleges, the universities, and the libraries, never forgetting in the process, however, that what makes museums different is, first of all, the objects, and second, an informal learning environment.

How have we put this all together into a national programme? The Smithsonian Kellogg Project began formally in 1982 with the creation of a National Advisory Committee comprising both museum professionals and staff from university continuing education programmes. Suffice it to say that, as a national programme, it was fairly easy to get breadth in the project; we selected representative museums from various regions around the country. Likewise with the matter of subject disciplines: we selected a representative mix of art, history, science, natural history, children's museums and living collection museums. The problem was to get some depth into the project, and that matter we dealt with by selecting, from some 486 applicant institutions, twelve museums — two from each of the six American Association of Museums' geographical regions — which committed themselves to participate with the Smithsonian in all aspects of the Kellogg Project over the next three years. Each museum put together a Project team, which had to include the museum director, and which would carry out Project ideas and activities on site. In this way we hoped to be able to track and analyze the process, or series of processes, by which museums might alter their ways of operating in order to make themselves more central to the educational life of their communities and regions.

The twelve museums selected were: the Museum of Science, Boston; the Rhode Island Black Heritage Society, Providence; the New York Botanical Garden, in the Bronx; the Carnegie Institute (both the Museum of Art and the Carnegie Museum of Natural History), Pittsburgh; the Science Museums of Charlotte, North Carolina; the Louisiana State Museum, New Orleans; the Toledo Museum of Art; the Children's Museum, Indianapolis; the San Antonio Museum Association, Texas, which includes the Witte Museum of History, the Museum of Art, and the Transportation Museum; the Cherokee National Museum, Tahlequah, Oklahoma; the Fine Arts Museums of San Francisco, which include the De Young Museum and the Palace of the Legion of Honor; and the Oregon Historical Society, in Portland, Oregon.

Three phases of activity are carried out by the Kellogg Project: the first brings together museum professionals to discuss key issues in improving the learning environment in museums; the second offers support to the participating museums to try new or different ways of pursuing educational programming; and the third encourages collaboration among museums and other educational institutions at the local, state, regional, and national levels.

The first phase, a discussion of issues, is carried out through national colloquia, regional workshops, and a residency programme.

Colloquium I, "Increasing the Museum's Responsiveness to Cultural Diversity", was held in April, 1983. It united for the first time two senior staff from each of the twelve museums selected to participate as full partners with the Smithsonian Institution during the three years of the Kellogg Project, and initiated a continuing philosophical dialogue on the relationships of museums to their diverse communities.

In October, 1984, the second colloquium, "Museums in Pursuit of Educational Excellence", was conducted to examine the possible impact of the "information age" on museums, how museums can inspire creativity and quality in their educational activities, and how museums can effect internal changes in order to improve public programmes. Teams from the twelve full participation museums attended the three-day colloquium.

The series of six regional workshops held in 1983-84 brought 120 additional museums into the Kellogg Project at a regional network level, twenty museums in each region being selected in order to widen the discussions begun at Colloquium I. These workshops functioned as a series of open forums, wherein senior museum professionals — directors, curators, educators, exhibit designers, and the like — met to discuss practical ways of making museums more central to learning in their communities.

The programme of the regional workshops was "Broadening the Museum's Educational

Role in its Community", and among the topics addressed were: expanding the public's access, both intellectual and physical, to a museum's learning resources — its collections, exhibitions, research activities, and staff expertise — and developing practical strategies for increasing the use of a museum's learning tools. These tools include demonstrations, study tours, lectures, courses, films, workshops, school kits and programmes, publications, and audio-visual productions. In round table and group discussions, participating senior museum professionals shared their experiences and expertise. Case studies from the Smithsonian and the two full participation museums in each region were presented; these were analyzed as key educational programmes and processes. As a result of these workshops, regional networks were formed that have continued these discussions; the workshops also encouraged collaborative efforts among museums and other educational institutions, and increased communication between museums and community, business and political leaders.

A special Smithsonian Kellogg Project workshop was held in January, 1985. Planned as an event to spearhead Kellogg Project research activities, the workshop featured Dr. Reuven Feuerstein, child psychologist from Israel, who is internationally known for his theories and teaching techniques based on the "mediated learning experience". Dr. Feuerstein is presently turning his professional attention to the subject of learning in museums, and at this workshop he presented his ideas to a group composed of museum educators from the Kellogg Project full participation museums, Smithsonian museums, and other museums, schools, and colleges in the Washington-Baltimore area.

Three Kellogg Project full participation museums plan to work with Dr. Feuerstein in developing research projects which relate to their demonstration programmes: one such project is already being developed by the Cherokee National Museum. Other specialized workshops for peer review and critique of demonstration programmes have been conducted at the New York Botanical Gardens and the San Francisco Art Museums.

Another major element of the "discussion phase" of the Kellogg Project has been a series of senior-level professional residencies held at the Smithsonian Institution.

The Kellogg Museum Professionals at the Smithsonian programme, as these residencies are called, is designed to enable museum decision-makers (directors and senior staff) to study and work with colleagues at the Smithsonian museums, investigating solutions to problems or issues in museum education drawn from their own institutions. Participants are selected from the 150 museum professionals who have attended Kellogg Project workshops, having thereby already discussed the key issues identified by the Kellogg Project. Residencies are ten days long, and an individualized programme of study is arranged for each resident, drawing on the collections, programmes, and staff of the Smithsonian museums and on other Washington cultural organizations. Residents participate in daily dialogue sessions on each other's topic of study, and each resident is required to reflect (in writing) on three museum objects, examining the relationship of objects to learning in the museum.

Although the original plan was to hold all Kellogg Project residencies at the Smithsonian Institution, it became apparent that a broader policy for residencies needed to be adopted if the residencies were to be truly useful to the twelve full participation museums. Accordingly, the concept of the residencies for these museums was expanded to include four options: (1) one or more Kellogg Project team members could have a regular short-term residency at the Smithsonian; (2) one or more team members could have a residency at a museum other than the Smithsonian, if work relevant to the Kellogg Project was taking place there; (3) a visiting expert or experts could be a resident at the team's home museum, to assist it with some phase of the Kellogg project; or (4) a residency could be put together by combining any of these options. In each case, the residency had to be directly related to the museum's demonstration programme.

What are the demonstration programmes? The demonstration programmes represent the second phase of the Smithsonian Kellogg Project activity — support of new or different ways of pursuing educational programming. Further, they are attempts to put into practice strategies discussed at the colloquia and workshops.

The twelve full participation museums reflect the Kellogg Project's working philosophies in their chosen demonstration programmes. Three museums are examining different aspects of developing new interpretations of existing collections and exhibitions.

The Children's Museum in Indianapolis is conducting a nationwide survey of the variety of techniques used by history museums to interpret historical artifacts for the public. Participatory exhibitions of traditional skills, "living history" presentations, and mixed media "Time Voyages" are among the exciting ideas with which the Children's Museum hopes to transform its Hall of History. The museum is also planning a 1986 national conference to explore, examine, and discuss "learning in museums".

The Cherokee National Museum in Tahlequah, Oklahoma, is planning to utilize oral history recording projects among elder Cherokee to gather stories of life in a Cherokee village at the turn-of-the-century. These real-life accounts will be used to develop a sound-and-light presentation which will interpret a number of authentic turn-of-the-century buildings in a recreated 1900 Cherokee village at the museum.

The Fine Arts Museums of San Francisco have established a whole range of educational activities to interpret the Teotihuacan wall murals from Mexico. Not only are the cultural and iconographic aspects of the murals examined but so are the conservation aspects, the conservation work being carried out right in the galleries with an international team of conservators. A bilingual student "ambassador" programme will bring these interpretations to a youthful Spanish speaking audience.

Three museums are concentrating on working more closely with elementary and secondary schools to increase the use of museum resources in teaching.

The San Antonio Museum Association, in conjunction with the local school system, is creating a Commission on School/Museum Partnerships. This commission will carry on activities at both the policy-making and teaching levels to ensure awareness and utilization of museum resources in curriculum planning and teacher training.

The Oregon Historical Society is attempting a similar programme on a statewide scale; it plans to involve other cultural institutions from around the state — colleges and universities, community arts organizations, and funding agencies — in order to demonstrate resource-sharing and co-ordination of educational programming.

The Science Museums of Charlotte, North Carolina, a museum complex charged with teaching science in conjunction with the city and county schools, is developing live dramatic presentations in which important figures in the history of science will explain scientific principles by carrying out the experiments that made them famous. Three presentations are currently planned: one on the behaviour of gases, one on developments in modern communication, and one an "Intergalactic Game Show," in which students test their knowledge of science against one another with the aid of a robot.

Three museums are reaching out into their communities through the establishment of new lifelong learning programmes.

The Toledo Museum of Art, which has pioneered adult educational offerings over the years, is studying the successes and failures of adult learning programmes in order to improve and expand such learning opportunities. Recognizing that adults learn in different ways than children, the museum is re-designing the orientation to its galleries in order to expand self-study for adults.

The Louisiana State Museum, recognizing its statewide responsibilities, will bring the museum to the public through television. Its programmes will focus in particular on adult/child interaction in museums, thereby encouraging family learning.

The Museum of Science in Boston is trying an innovative marketing plan to identify the interest of its "consumers" (those who use the museum and its resources) in order to adapt its "products" (its exhibitions and educational programs) to the needs of the community.

The final three museums are involved in interaction, collaboration, and networking.

The Carnegie Institute in Pittsburgh consists of two museums, the Museum of Art and the Carnegie Museum of Natural History, which, although existing under the same roof for over ninety years, have never worked together on a joint project.

Not only will the Carnegie's programme seek to demonstrate the process by which two cultural institutions can overcome innate barriers to collaborate on joint ventures, but it will also demonstrate how cross-fertilization from two different subject areas — in this case art and natural history — can enrich subjects.

The New York Botanical Garden, located in the Bronx for nearly a century, has long served an educated community in greater New York; it now desires to establish closer ties with its immediate neighbourhood. To do this, the Garden plans to establish a community advisory group which will assist in developing extension programmes and services in which the local residents, many of whom are disadvantaged, can participate.

The Rhode Island Black Heritage Society, of Providence, has literally reached into its own community to find its resources — the artifacts, the documents, the family stories, the histories of black churches, business, fraternal, and political organizations – and in the process has uncovered more information about Black America than was thought to exist. The Society is now giving this information back to its community through exhibitions, concerts, and celebratory festivals to demonstrate that knowledge of one's past creates individual worth, ethnic pride, and community fellowship.

Finally, we arrive at the third phase of Kellogg Project activity, encouraging collaboration and networking among museums and other educational institutions at all levels. Having participants in the Kellogg workshops be eligible for participation in residencies at the Smithsonian has greatly encouraged networking among a wide variety of American museums. The Kellogg Project has also increased collaboration between the Smithsonian Institution and other museums. Workshops have brought together museum personnel and personnel from other types of cultural and educational institutions.

How will the fruits of the colloquia, the workshops, the residencies, and the twelve demonstration programmes be shared with the rest of the museum profession, allowing others to profit from these experiences as they develop their own programmes? A two-fold process of evaluation and dissemination is helping to assess Kellogg Project results and spread them abroad.

Evaluation is an essential part of every Kellogg Project activity, not only as process, but as example. Philip Spiess, Coordinator of the Smithsonian Kellogg Project, has said, "Through my travels to various museums and during our workshops, I have found to

my surprise and consternation, that the museum profession in the United States is constantly looking for two things – "quick fixes" to problems, and more money. The feeling is "if we only had more money, we could do much more," and "Give us an instant formula for a good educational programme, so we don't have to waste our time thinking about it". Well, we all know things don't work this way: money without imagination and creativity will improve nothing; likewise, if an institution will not consider its own particular resources, mission, needs, and audience when developing its programmes, a programme that has been successful elsewhere will not help it.

This is where evaluation comes in. What each institution needs most, and what many institutions seem to avoid, is effective self-analysis, not for congratulations or for criticism, but for the staff to think about what they do, why they do it, how it contributes to the work of the institution, and how it contributes to the life of the community. The dual life of the museum – its internal life, that is, how it organizes itself and how it functions, and its external life, that is, its intimate relationship with its audience and its community – should be the prime concern, for thought, for examination, and for action. Professional evaluation can assist in this process.

The original grant from the W.K. Kellogg Foundation to the Smithsonian Institution was a three-year grant. As we neared the end of the third year, however, it became apparent that we were really only at the mid-point of achieving what we had set out to do. The first year had been one of planning, the second, one of establishing programmes, and the third, one of implementing programmes. Evaluation and dissemination of the Project results remained to be done. This suggested a two-year extension to the Project which has now been approved by the Kellogg Foundation.

While evaluation has been an integral part of the Kellogg Project from the beginning — a professional museum evaluator, Dr. Robert Wolf, of Indiana University, is on contract with the Kellogg Project — we must look, in the next two years, at the more long-range effects of the Kellogg Project and its activities, what impact it has had over time. Likewise, the effects of the twelve demonstration programmes must be studied. We hope also to get data on how the Smithsonian Kellogg Project has influenced activities in museums which have not participated directly in the Kellogg Project.

If evaluation of results of the Kellogg Project is important, it is likewise important to disseminate these results, in order to ensure that the Kellogg Project has the broadest possible impact among museums and other community institutions interested in education. Some dissemination is already taking place; it will be carried out through the following activities: national conferences, which will respond to the key issues which have emerged from the Kellogg Project; workshops and seminars, which will present the demonstration programmes for illustration and critical review by colleagues; professional residencies, which will build upon and expand the Kellogg Project findings; publications, including research reports, proceedings of the national meetings and colloquia and a summary report of Kellogg Project findings; and, finally, a videotape series, illustrating the role of learning in museums and demonstrating the use of museums as community learning centres.

The course of the Smithsonian Kellogg Project has not been an easy one. But, by remaining flexible and altering our direction as circumstances have warranted it, we have continued to try to urge the museum profession in the United States to expand beyond the traditional, the tried, and the tired. What the Smithsonian Kellogg Project has done for American museums we feel can be done elsewhere as well, our philosophical tenets apply to any museum, and the sorts of programmes we have developed can be replicated anywhere.

Learning has no end — and the potential use of museums as learning resources likewise is unlimited. Museums — repositories of the past — can serve the future through their unique learning opportunity: the opportunity for people to come into touch with lives that went before, through contact with the living products of those lives.

Museums for the 21st Century

Lawrence L. Reger

Lawrence L. Reger has been, since 1978, Director of
the American Association of Museums, an
organisation with over 10,000 museum and personal
members and with a budget of over $2 million. The
Association's most recent major initiative has been its
Commission on Museums for a New Century — a
far-sighted study on the future of museums.

I assume that the principle reason I was invited to speak to your conference was the publication last Autumn by the American Association of Museums of *Museums for a New Century*. It was interesting to me that I was asked to discuss "Museums for the 21st Century".

My presumption is, whether consciously or unconsciously, the distinction between the use of "new" and "21st" to designate the next century reflects in some measure the differing outlook of how our two countries perceive the advancing of time. Because the vast majority of the descendants of our country came within the last 200 years we view the beginning of a new century not so much as a continuum but something "new". On the other hand, the documented history of your country and its culture spans many centuries.

I suspect that this difference in attitude may also reflect a difference in how we will approach the development of our museums in the next 10 to 15 years. I hope that my remarks will serve to stimulate discussion on this important topic.

The report of the Commission on Museums for a New Century culminated almost three years of work. The commission was established because we felt that it was important for museums to begin to look ahead and what better benchmark than the approaching 21st century?

We felt that if done well such an effort could serve museums both in the immediate and long term as they seek to improve their programmes, services and administration. It could also help museums secure the financial resources they need.

Financial resources are essential to the success of museums and tend to preoccupy the attention of museum professionals, trustees and others concerned about museums. However, before addressing this issue the members of the commission felt it was important for the work of the commission to consider (1) the forces of change in the broader society that are likely to impact on museums, (2) the broad goals and objectives of museums regarding their two basic concerns — collections and learning, and (3) the need for museums to work together and with other organizations and groups.

Museums for a New Century is intended to be a tool that can be used to improve a museum's programmes and services. It was also intended to encourage discussion about the future of museums.

The principal criticism of the commission report to date has been by those who feel that there was not a sufficient amount of attention given to particular areas of concern. For example, several people have noted that there is not much discussion about the international dimension of museums. I believe they make a good case. The report in my opinion could have addressed this area in more detail.

Before turning to some specific aspects of the commission's work I would like to comment briefly on the process. There were 24 members of the commission representing the broad spectrum of kinds of museums, everything from art museums to zoos. Also included were education, foundation and business representatives.

At its initial meetings there was scepticism expressed by museum directors on the commission that enough common ground could be found between the different kinds of museums to produce a meaningful report. When the process was completed many of the participants were of the opinion that the single most important benefit of the commission's work will be the development of a much stronger sense of community and ultimately co-operation between museums of all kinds and sizes in our country. There are, of course, differences among kinds and sizes of museums that must be addressed and many are highlighted in the commission's

report. However, the things that museums have in common are ultimately more important.

The report recommends two priorities for action − the growth, organization and care of museum collections and the function of museums as institutions of learning. Eight of the 16 recommendations are concerned with these two areas. The remainder of the recommendations propose avenues for taking action. They include extending collaborative efforts with other museums and other kinds of institutions, increasing public awareness of the essential services museums provide, and working toward long-term financial stability.

The report highlights seven specific conditions in museums that need to be approached with fresh insight. These are the key issues that must be addressed, if museums in our country are to thrive and be meaningful institutions in our society as we approach the next century. I would like to review and comment on each of these.

First, the commission noted that "there are pressing needs with regard to the growth, organization and care of museum collections. Museum staff, trustees and supporters must turn closer attention to the current and future condition of objects that are the heart of our museums".

Early in the work of the commission it became apparent that care of collections was an issue that needed to be addressed in the coming years on a signficantly greater scale than had previously been the case. It was also an issue that lent itself to and required a nationwide co-ordinated programme. While the commission was still completing its work, the American Association of Museums began to focus attention on various aspects of care of collections. To further this effort we have worked with our Congress and federal agencies that support museums, which include the Institute of Museum Services, National Endowment for the Arts, National Endowment for the Humanities and National Science Foundation.

Our goal is to significantly increase care of collections as a priority with museums and public and private agencies that support them. Shortly after the release of the commission report we published a brochure entitled "Caring for Collections" that was funded by the National Endowment for the Humanities. While this report is limited to collections specifically related to the humanities, the overall recommendations apply to collections of all kinds. The report concluded that the priorities of the museum community should be to:
— improve environmental conditions for collections
— inventory, register and catalogue objects to achieve documentary control of collections
— conserve objects within collections
— expand knowledge through in-depth research on collections and enhance public understanding of museum collections through the dissemination of information about them.

We have just recently completed a comprehensive statistical survey of collections of museums of all kinds. It reveals that 5% of the collections are in serious need of treatment. Serious need was defined as objects being in danger of partial or complete loss unless treated soon. Perhaps more important, the condition of 40% of the collections was identified as unknown. Further, 72% of the museums report that they have no written long-range plan or policy for the care of their collections.

We have had considerable success in gaining recognition of the importance of the collections in all the museums in our country. One of the most gratifying moments in my tenure as director of the American Association of Museums came last year when Congressman Sidney Yates addressed our annual meeting. Mr Yates is chair of the Congressional committee responsible for making recommendations on appropriations for the Institute of Museum Services and the Arts and Humanities Endowments. He said:

"The national parks were just about the first national conservation areas. After having set aside Yosemite and Yellowstone National Parks, Congress passed legislation establishing the park system, and it's interesting to note how applicable that legislation might be for museums today. It provided for: 'the conservation of the scenery and natural and historical objects, the wildlife and for the enjoyment of the same in such manner and by such means as will leave them unimpaired for future generations.'

"We are moving more and more toward conservation and preservation, to recognition of the importance of protecting our resources and artifacts for future generations. We are taking care of our parks, our forests, our wilderness areas, our wild and scenic rivers, our historic buildings, our archeological discoveries. We have a national register of historic places and we have legislation protecting landmarks. We still have not taken the steps we should to protect the historic and irreplaceable objects in our museums.

"The magnificence of our nation's museum collections is incredible and overwhelming. So many museums have great treasures that must be preserved for future generations. Their loss would be irretrievable."

We have also been successful in securing federal funds to address collections maintenance and documentation. As I am sure you can appreciate this was no easy task in light of the Reagan administration's efforts to reduce domestic programmes. This in turn has helped to secure increased support for museums from private sources, as well as state and local governments.

The second priority of the commission states that "museums have not realized their full potential as educational institutions. Despite a long-standing and serious commitment to their function as institutions of informal learning, there is a troublesome gap between reality and potential that must be addressed by policy makers in education and museums." There are four specific recommendations of the commission in the area of learning. This is more than on any other issue.

From my perspective one of the most important factors is one of credibility. Specifically, are those in museums and the general public really convinced that museums play an important role in learning? The term "*informal* learning" that is used in the commission report was carefully chosen. It is generally recognized that individuals are most receptive to learning when they are motivated in a positive way. In other words, when they are enjoying themselves. Yet there still persists in our country, probably a hangover from our puritan heritage, a notion that education is a duty and something that is done in a serious

way — that too often translates into something that is accomplished in a stifling atmosphere.

First, museum professionals themselves must be convinced of the importance of the role that museums play in learning. They must be more positive and self-assured about what museums have to offer.

Then we must generate the same appreciation on the part of leaders in formal education, namely our schools, and then the general public. This will not be an easy task. It is one that probably has to come principally from the local rather than national level.

Research into the ways that people learn in museums, examination of how museums and schools can better co-operate, and examination of ways that museums can serve the adult public as sources of intellectual enrichment are all important steps in addressing this priority.

Turning now to what must be done to help museums address these two goals, the commission identified as central to the future of our museums the role of governing authorities. The commission report states that "the times demand strong, forward-thinking leadership from museums. Their organizational structure, in particular their system of governance, needs re-examination to ensure that it will meet the demands of the future." The commission recommended that a task force be assembled to assess the quality of governance of American museums, examining such matters as board/staff relationships and the selection and composition of boards.

More than two-thirds of our museums are private not-for-profit institutions that are governed by boards of trustees composed of individuals who volunteer their time and services. Even in the case of museums that are part of a state or local government, there are very often advisory boards made up of private citizens and while the ultimate legal responsibility does not rest with these advisory boards their recommendations are almost always accepted.

The ideal relationship between trustees and staff is stated in our handbook for museum trustees: "Museum trustees make policy . . . and monitor the execution of that policy . . . Although trustees are ultimately responsible for the museum, they must remain aloof from the actual execution of its day-to-day operations."

The application, or misapplication, of this principle is the central issue facing our system of museum governance. The ground rules are not clear about what constitutes "policy" and how narrow or broad policy-making authority should be. When there is confusion, misunderstanding or a conflict, it most often involves culpability on the part of both the governing authority – trustees – and museum professionals.

This situation is due in large measure to the historical development of museums in our country. Most of our museums were founded and initially operated by volunteers. Many of our smaller museums still do not have professional staff and volunteers continue to play an important role in larger museums. This is at one and the same time both a strength and weakness. We could not accomplish what we do without the help of individuals who give freely of their time. Alexis de Toqueville long ago noted that our

attraction for voluntary organizations borders on a fixation when he said:

> "Americans of all ages, all conditions, and all dispositions constantly form associations. They have not only commercial and manufacturing companies, in which all take part, but associations of a thousand other kinds, religious, moral, serious, futile, general or restricted, enormous or diminutive . . . if it is proposed to inculcate some truth or to foster some feelings by the encouragement of a great example, they form a society. Wherever at the head of some new undertaking you see the government in France, or a man of rank in England, in the United States you will be sure to find an association."

Another important factor is that trustees have the major responsibility for raising funds to support a museum. As part of this responsibility they must understand in some depth the use to which the funds will be put. Inevitably, personal interests and concerns and sometimes differences with the staff surface not only as priorities but specifics.

The commission report notes that "old rules are changing; just as the job of museum director is no longer genteel employment, so the position of trustee is no longer just a source of social cachet. Today's trustee must be knowledgeable about the functions of the museum, in tune with the needs and interests of its constituencies, and committed to ensuring the museum's financial stability".

There is a concensus that our system of lay governance is ultimately the best for our institutions. The goal must be to make it work better. We need to perfect the partnership of trustees and staff that can offer strong, co-operative and forward-thinking leadership. Both are working in the same institutions and towards the same mission.

The AAM's Trustee Committee offers a good model for addressing this issue. The committee is composed of trustees of museums throughout the United States. It provides workshops for its members, a newsletter and other publications and participates in our annual meeting by sponsoring panel sessions in co-operation with other committees, such as curators, educators and public relations. This work should be significantly expanded to provide more programmes at the regional and local level. New ones are also needed such as a consultancy programme that would make available one or two individuals knowledgeable and experienced in museum governance to work with a board and staff.

The next of the seven conditions that I would like to single out relates to the one that I have just been discussing. The commission states that "the diversity of the community of museums is not fully representative of the diversity of the society it seeks to serve. In their governance and staffing, museums have much to gain by making a commitment to greater diversity".

The "diversity" referred to is the varied cultural and ethnic groups in our society. Looking to the future more than half of the population growth in our country in the next two decades will come from minorities. By the year 2000, 20% of our population will be black or Hispanic. In the same time frame, the number of Asians in our population will double from close to 4 million to nearly 8 million.

The commission placed special emphasis on the importance of strengthening smaller museums whose purpose it is to serve these groups. It also encouraged greater collaboration between small and large museums as a way of better serving minority groups. These two approaches were recommended as the best approach to addressing this issue rather than urging larger museums to make significant changes in their purposes.

The commission also noted the need for increasing representation of minorities in the museum workforce at all levels and the under-representation of women in higher levels of management as an important challenge that must be addressed. The solution, it was agreed, will not come quickly. However, steps must be taken. For example, museums working with educational institutions are urged to explore ways of interesting minority young people in museum work. There are examples of programmes in other sectors, such as higher education, that could be adopted to provide opportunities for women to advance to more responsible positions.

How museums are perceived by the general public, especially leaders in the private and public sector, represents another important consideration which the commission recommended as an area that must be addressed. The chapter dealing with this issue is entitled, "From Private Appreciation to Public Awareness". The report notes that "again and again this commission has encountered a deep private appreciation for individual museums, their collections and the multi-faceted museum experience . . . But the rich personal meanings with which museums are endowed are curiously unrelated to their collective public image, an image often encumbered by cliches".

The private experience, which is often casual and relatively unstructured, is one of a museum's most important assets and must be preserved. The challenge is how do we translate this into support by the general public for our museums? The casual nature of the museum experience is too often reflected in a casual or superficial understanding of the roles and responsibilities of museums and their needs.

We need to improve the collective image of our museums. Almost every segment of our society has a public relations programme. Newspapers, radio and television and replete with messages from the dairy farmer, insurance industry and even the defence establishment. The same is not true of museums. How people perceive museums determines how much and how well they use them, and ultimately, how fully they support them.

Our Association in conjunction with the Institute for Museum Services and the President's Committee on the Arts and Humanities will sponsor a nationwide programme in the Autumn of 1987 to encourage individuals and corporations to "Invest in America's Collections". Sears Roebuck, our nation's largest consumer retailer and its stockbrokerage affiliate, Dean Witter, have agreed to take the lead as the private sponsor. Not only will this programme offer an opportunity for all museums to raise funds but it will, we hope, be a first step towards generating a broader understanding by the public of museums.

Contributing to the lack of a broad appreciation for the work of museums is the fact that there are no comprehensive statistics available about museums in our country. There have been two nationwide surveys that were done in 1972 and 1979, however, they were not followed up with additional surveys, which would highlight changes. The commission noted this and then said, "as a mature and public profession, the museum field has an obligation to set up a mechanism for continuously analyzing data about museums".

The collections study that I mentioned earlier is our Association's first attempt to address this issue. This was a study requested by the Congress of the United States and funded through the Institute of Museum Services. The National Endowment for the Arts is working with us to develop a feasibility study for a periodic survey of museums. This is needed not only to provide reliable information for the public but also for individual museums who need it in order to do responsible planning.

The last of the seven conditions enumerated by the commission describes the economic situations of museums as extremely fragile. The report states that "future economic stability is an issue that both museums and their supporters must address, for financial health is essential if museums are to fulfill their responsibilities and satisfy the expectations society holds for them".

Let me try to put the cost of keeping museums running on a day-to-day basis in perspective as best we can with the limited information that we have. This does not include capital expenses, such as acquisition of collections, construction and endowment or other permanent funds which generate interest income from their corpus.

The 1979 survey of museums reported total operating budgets of $784 million for the 4,214 museums participating. By extrapolating, the study concluded that there were as many as 5,000 museums with total budgets in the order of $1 billion. While we do not have reliable current figures, I would be willing to estimate that budgets of museums are now approaching $1.5 billion. While this is a considerable amount, it must be put in perspective. For example, our country's gross national product was $3,662,800 million in 1984.

The title of the chapter of the commission report dealing with the financial needs of museums is "The Economic Picture — A Joint Venture". That summarizes the situation that has developed over the last several decades in our country, namely that increasingly museums are seeking support from both private and public sources. Museums that traditionally secured their support from governmental entities are now including fund-raising campaigns to interest individuals, foundations and corporations in supporting them. On the other hand, museums that have been privately supported are seeking to augment their support from our federal government as well as local and state governments.

In addition, most museums have placed a greater emphasis on earned income. Admission charges, museum shops and restaurant facilities are now the rule rather the exception.

I would be remiss if I did not mention what has become known as the "blockbuster" exhibition, which has generated a great deal of discussion both within and without the museum community. It is clear that museums, especially larger ones, have made this kind of exhibition a part of their on-going programme.

John Russell, a critic for the *New York Times* did one of the best analyses of this phenomenon that I have seen. He concluded that "blockbusters" provide many of our citizens with an opportunity to see important objects that they would not otherwise be able to see, that the best of the exhibitions contribute to the scholarship of a particular field and that as is the case with any kind of activity these can be models. One of the important concerns that each museum must address is to keep the resources for these major projects from deterring other important work.

This approach to funding our museums has been called "pluralistic". It has developed out of necessity. On the whole I believe that it has been good for museums. It broadens the interest in them. It does require that more human and financial resources be devoted to securing income.

Museums must become even more aggressive in their efforts to obtain necessary financial resources. Fund-raising must not, however, be an end in itself. That is why this important subject was left to the last chapter of *Museums for a New Century.* We must be clear about our goals and objectives and forceful in articulating the roles and responsibilities of our institutions.

Whether the commission's recommendations are the correct approach to meeting the challenges of the future remains to be seen. The real test of its work will be whether it contributes to helping the museums of our country to achieve their potential to serve society in the next century.

Printed in Scotland for HMSO by McQueen Printers, Galashiels.
Dd. 0762165 C15 4/86.